Aung San Suu Kyi

Aung San Suu Kyi

Fearless Voice of Burma

WHITNEY STEWART

⌊ Lerner Publications Company/Minneapolis

Other books by Whitney Stewart

The 14th Dalai Lama: Spiritual Leader of Tibet
Sir Edmund Hillary: To Everest and Beyond

Lerner Publications Company
A division of Lerner Publishing Group
241 First Avenue North
Minneapolis, Minnesota 55401 U.S.A.

Website address: www.lernerbooks.com

Library of Congress Cataloging-in-Publication Data

Stewart, Whitney, 1959–
    Aung San Suu Kyi : fearless voice of Burma / Whitney Stewart.
        p. cm.
    Includes bibliographical references and Index.
    Summary: A biography of the Burmese leader who won the Nobel Peace Prize in 1991 while under house arrest.
    ISBN 0–8225–4931–X (lib. bdg. : alk. paper)
    1. Aung San Suu Kyi—Juvenile literature. 2. Burma—Politics and government—1988—Juvenile literature. 3. Burma—Politics and government—1948—Juvenile literature. 4. Democracy—Burma—Juvenile literature. 5. Politicians—Burma—Biography—Juvenile literature. [1. Aung San Suu Kyi. 2. Politicians. 3. Women—Biography. 4. Burma—Politics and government—1948– 5. Burma—Politics and government—1988–] I. Title.
DS530.53.A85S74 1997
959.105'092–dc20
[B]   96–41812

Manufactured in the United States of America
2 3 4 5 6 7 – JR – 06 05 04 03 02 01

ACKNOWLEDGMENTS

For reasons of security, I cannot mention the names of many people I interviewed. I hope they will know I am grateful for their help.

Aung San Suu Kyi and her secretary, U Aye Win, were gracious to squeeze me into Daw Suu Kyi's very tight schedule. U Aye Win is now in prison for speaking to journalists about Aung San Suu Kyi. Aung San Suu Kyi kindly answered my questions and those I posed on behalf of Billie Andersson's 1995 enrichment classes at the Trinity Episcopal School of New Orleans.

There are four Burmese people without whom I could not have written this biography: U Kyaw Win, Zarni, Khin Ohmar, and Soe Pyne. The first person to introduce me to the personal side of Aung San Suu Kyi was Marlee Clymer. Marlee's insights inspired me.

No book is ever written by one person alone. The following people have woven themselves into my pages: Neil Alexander, Christiane Andersson, Lütte Andersson, Simon Billenness, Ethan Casey, Kenton Clymer, Bob DeBellevue, Elise Diament, Cindy Dike, Larry Dohrs, Marigny Dupuy, Cynthia and John Everets, Julie Ford, Audrey Freid, Bob Fuller, Patricia Herbert, Pwint Htun, Sarah Krakauer, Timothy Landon, Lloyd Lear, Vickie Lewelling, Daniel and Linda Lorenzetti, Arlette Martin, Ken Molony, Jim Mooring, Stu Nagurka, Nyi Nyi Aung, Deborah Oppenheim, Mary Pack, Bill Richardson, Inge Sargent, Carlin and George Scherer, Ms. Seng Raw, Richard Stewart, Strider, Celie Stumm, Jenny Tun Aung, Tom Varisco, Robert Williams, Dr. Sein Win, Lobsang Yeshi, and Zaw Zaw.

I cannot say enough about the brilliance of my editor, Susan Breckner Rose, picture editor, Nancy Smedstad, and designer, Zachary Marell.

Finally, I want to thank my husband, Hans Andersson, and my son, Christoph Andersson, for taking care of each other while I was in Burma, and for supporting me while I researched and wrote this book.

—WS

To the people of Burma

CONTENTS

Aung San Suu Kyi waits in her childhood home in Rangoon, Burma.

CHAPTER ONE

SILENCING THE LEADERS

ON THE MORNING OF JULY 20, 1989, AUNG SAN Suu Kyi (ahng sahn soo chee) woke up in her childhood home in Rangoon, the capital of Burma. One of her cousins came over from his house across the street. "Something is happening," he said. "There are lots of soldiers all over the place outside."

Many Burmese people had recently been arrested and jailed by Burma's military rulers for supporting a democratic movement led by the National League for Democracy (NLD). Suu Kyi knew she could go to prison. She was the NLD general secretary. What would happen to her two sons if she was taken away? How would her husband, Michael, find her when he arrived from England?

Quickly and calmly, Suu Kyi organized herself. Her sons, eleven-year-old Kim and sixteen-year-old Alexander, were with her on holiday from England. She arranged for a friend to care for the boys until Michael arrived. Suu Kyi said that they all "had gotten quite used to people being taken away and put into prison, so I packed a small bag."

Not allowing herself to feel afraid or angry, Suu Kyi waited with Alexander, Kim, and some friends. The boys played games with the student activists staying in Suu Kyi's compound, and the adults chatted cheerfully. All of them were determined to help Burma through the national elections the military government had promised it would hold the following spring. "We had quite a merry time because there were a lot of friends here," Suu Kyi said.

After some time, the son of Tin Oo, the NLD chairperson, came over. He told them that his father "was going out for one of his usual morning walks this morning and soldiers told him he was not allowed to go out."

Suu Kyi presumed that she too was a prisoner in her own house. She did not even try to go out. Truckloads of government soldiers barricaded her front gate. Friends could still come in, however, and they joined Suu Kyi to discuss events and eat lunch with her. Nothing unusual happened for several hours.

At about four o'clock in the afternoon, an official of the State Law and Order Restoration Council (SLORC) entered Suu Kyi's home with a crowd of military officers. They read a detention order to Suu Kyi, and then they began to search the house. Kim asked his mother if the men were going to take her away. She explained to him that she would be locked up in the compound.

Armed Burmese soldiers are on the lookout from guard houses outside of Aung San Suu Kyi's compound.

Some friends stayed with Suu Kyi and the boys during the house search, which lasted until four o'clock in the morning. Only Kim fell asleep out of exhaustion.

"They took away masses and masses of papers," Suu Kyi remembered. "And then everybody was taken away and I was left with the two children."

When Michael Aris, who was attending his father's funeral in Scotland, heard that his wife had been put under house arrest, he immediately flew to Burma. Stepping off the plane at Rangoon's airport, he saw that his plane was surrounded by soldiers. He was immediately escorted away by a military officer. The British embassy official sent to meet Michael had no idea what had happened to him. Michael said: "For twenty-two days I effectively disappeared from sight. Nobody knew what had happened to me. The British press carried stories about how an Oxford don [professor] had gone missing. My family in England was extremely worried. The British government and the European Community pressed very hard for . . . contact, but to no avail. I had vanished."

To join his wife and sons, Michael had to agree to the strict terms already imposed on his wife. He was forced to promise to avoid any contact with embassy personnel and with people active in politics. He was then delivered to Suu Kyi's home. Still, no one in England knew where he was.

Michael found his wife on a hunger strike. She had stopped eating on the day of her arrest because she wanted to ensure the decent treatment of the NLD supporters who had been taken away from her compound. She even asked to be jailed with them, because she believed that her presence would keep the jailers from treating the others harshly. After twelve days of her fasting, a military officer finally gave his word that the students would not be tortured and would have fair trials. Suu Kyi then broke her fast. Nobody knew whether the military government kept its promise.

Michael, Alexander, and Kim stayed with Suu Kyi for the next six weeks, until they had to leave for England to get back to school. More than two years would pass before the boys would see their mother again.

Michael leaves Rangoon with Kim (right) and Alexander in September to return to England.

Crowds of Burmese gather to listen to General Aung San.

SKIES THAT MOURNED

AUNG SAN SUU KYI'S FATHER WAS BURMA'S
beloved General Aung San. Most Burmese adored him.
Some politicians, however, were envious of his fame and
political power. They thought of him as an opportunist
whose political views changed regularly. Others tried to
align themselves with Aung San to share his glory.

In 1915, Aung San was born a son of "rural gentry and
patriots" from Natmauk, in central Burma. He grew up in
a Buddhist family full of social leaders and brilliant aca-
demics. After finishing high school in Natmauk, Aung
San attended Rangoon University. There he studied English literature, history, and social sciences. He began to
study law but became so involved in politics that he
never finished his degree. While still in school, Aung San
was suspended for fighting for student rights. After he returned to campus, he helped found and then became
president of Rangoon University Students' Union. He

also wrote articles for the English and Burmese newspapers and became an editor of *New Burma,* the only Eng-
lish-language paper managed by Burmese.

In 1938, Aung San joined the *Dobama Asi-ayone,* the
only nationalistic party in Burma at that time. Party
members were keen on forcing the British—who held
Burma as one of their colonies—out of Burma. After serv-
ing on several radical committees that were against the
British presence, Aung San went into hiding and began a
secret operation in August 1940. He was searching for a
foreign government willing to help the Burmese fight the
British so Burma could gain its independence.

Aung San traveled to China. Amid its own political up-
heavals, China seemed like a good prospect for support.
But after two months of trying to make political contacts
in China, Aung San found no support. Some agents of the
Japanese government, however, offered their assistance.
Although Aung San didn't completely trust the Japanese,
he believed they were the only ones who could force the
British out of Burma. He traveled to Japan, where the
Japanese government promised they would help Burma
become independent.

In early 1941, Aung San returned to Burma and re-
cruited the "Thirty Comrades" to take military training
with the Japanese. The Thirty Comrades became the
backbone of the Burma Independence Army (BIA), which
was formed in Thailand in December 1941. When the
Japanese forces moved into lower Burma in January 1942,
the BIA advanced from Thailand. One of the BIA's Thirty

Aung San Suu Kyi's father, Aung San

Comrades, a man named Ne Win, was heralded for reaching Rangoon and organizing internal battles against the British. Although in the same army, Aung San and Ne Win were not good friends.

In March 1942, the Japanese won a victory in the war against the British, and the British retreated. A Burmese man named Ba Maw became prime minister. Aung San became minister of defense and commander of the army.

Aung San fell sick while fighting against the British and went to Rangoon General Hospital to be treated in

1942. Known for his moodiness, hot temper, and some-times unrefined manners, Aung San frightened many people on the hospital staff. But the senior staff nurse, Daw Khin Kyi, handled him well. Her no-nonsense manner and good humor won the respect of Aung San. The two became easy friends, and their friendship led quickly to marriage. Daw Khin Kyi was just the right woman to share Aung San's politically active life.

General Aung San and Daw Khin Kyi were married in 1942.

Burma's sudden sense of success was short-lived. The Japanese were worse oppressors than the British. The Japanese had used the BIA to gain domination of Southeast Asia. As World War II was escalating, Japan wanted to block the Burma Road so that India could not send supplies to China. Both China and India had joined the Allied forces, including Britain and the United States, in fighting World War II.

The Japanese pretended to grant independence to Burma, and Aung San went along with the charade. He was not fooled, however. He was invited to Japan and decorated by the Japanese emperor, but he secretly planned a resistance against the Japanese.

At the end of 1944, Aung San turned back to the British and the other Allied forces fighting World War II, for help against the Japanese. Of course, some of the British wanted to imprison Aung San for treachery. Others decided that they could work with Aung San. One of those was Lord Louis Mountbatten, supreme Allied commander in Southeast Asia, who believed British colonial rule in Asia would soon end. Mountbatten knew Aung San was a natural leader and well loved by the Burmese. Aung San had earned the trust of many of Burma's ethnic minorities—including the Arakanese, Chins, Kachins, Karens, Mons, and Shans—as well as the religious minorities—Christians, Hindus, and Muslims.

Even Aung San's British opponent, Governor Reginald Dorman-Smith, admitted that Aung San was extremely popular: "We must, I think, accept it as fact that Aung

San is the most important figure in Burma today. Everyone appears to trust him and to admire him. . . . His troops adore him and will do anything he says. . . . If there were to be an election in Burma now and Aung San were to lead a party, it is generally considered that he would sweep the country."

On March 27, 1945, the Burmese army—led by General Aung San—revolted against the Japanese and joined the Allied forces. Less than three months later, on Tuesday, June 19, 1945, Aung San Suu Kyi was born in Rangoon. She was Aung San and Daw Khin Kyi's third child. Her name, *Aung San* for her father, *Suu* for her paternal grandmother, and *Kyi* for her mother, means "a bright collection of strange victories." Some Burmese believe that her name foreshadowed events in her life, and that her destiny was set at birth.

On August 15, 1945, the Japanese surrendered to the Allied forces. Aung San and his colleagues had to work with the British government again. Burma had been hit hard during the war, and there was much to rebuild. The British themselves were in disagreement over how to handle Burma. Former Governor Dorman-Smith wanted his power and position back, and he wanted Aung San arrested. Mountbatten wanted to move slowly—to assure the loyalty of Burmese soldiers, retrain the police, and check any opposition. He also knew that the country would revolt if Aung San were jailed.

In 1946, Daw Khin Kyi gave birth to another girl. This child lived for only a few days. Aung San and Daw Khin

Kyi lived with their two sons, Aung San U and Aung San Lin, and daughter, Aung San Suu Kyi, in a colonial house tucked away on a quiet road near Rangoon's Royal Lakes. Their house stood on a wooded hill, but the serenity of the landscape hid the activity inside their home. Politicians, scholars, soldiers, friends, and relatives all congregated there and filled the house with animated thought

Aung San Suu Kyi (left) and her two brothers pose with Aung San outside of their house near Rangoon's Royal Lakes.

Aung San Suu Kyi (bottom), *with her parents and brothers*

and dialogue. Husband and wife worked together to maintain a stable home, despite Burma's political confusion.

The Burmese felt no closer to independence, and most workers, beginning with the police, went on strike. The result was chaos, and the British caved in. Finally, Dorman-Smith was replaced by a new governor who shared Mountbatten's positive view of Aung San. With Burma under new leadership, Aung San joined the governing body and began to organize a plan for independence. Aung San had the support of the ethnic minorities in Burma, who believed that he could hold the entire country together. On January 27, 1947, Aung San and his delegation traveled to England to sign a treaty with the British.

The Aung San-Attlee Agreement offered Burma elections within four months and full independence within one year. The Burmese believed they would finally gain independence. They could cast their ballots for their own leader. The favored candidate was Aung San.

On the morning of July 19, 1947, a green army jeep stopped outside the secretariat building in downtown Rangoon. Inside, Aung San was holding a meeting with the executive committee of the interim government. Several men carrying semi-automatic weapons jumped out of the jeep and hurried into the building and upstairs to the meeting room. As the men charged into the room, Aung San stood up. The men yelled, "Remain seated. Don't move."

> AUNG SAN IS THE MOST IMPORTANT FIGURE IN BURMA TODAY. EVERYONE APPEARS TO TRUST HIM AND TO ADMIRE HIM.

With that, the men fired their weapons for about thirty seconds. Then they ran downstairs, out the door, and zoomed off in their jeep. Hired by U Saw, an envious political opponent of Aung San's, the assassins killed nine men. Seven of these men, including Aung San, were the most important leaders of the country.

The country mourned. Some people remember the day as dark and stormy, and they say that the skies also mourned. Aung San would never see the independence he had imagined. The country lost the man it trusted, and Aung San's three children lost their beloved father.

Daw Khin Kyi with her children, (left to right), Aung San U, Suu Kyi, and Aung San Lin

CHAPTER THREE

A STOIC FAMILY

WITH THE DEATH OF HER HUSBAND, DAW KHIN Kyi did not reveal her emotions. She had known she could lose her husband at any time. Daw Than E, a close family friend, described Daw Khin Kyi's reaction on the day of the assassination: "When news came of [her husband] being shot, she would not let a tear escape."

Facing parenthood alone, Daw Khin Kyi instilled in her children a strong memory of their father. She carefully considered what Aung San would have wanted for them. Suu Kyi was only two when her father died, so she learned about him mostly from family tales.

Daw Khin Kyi never encouraged her children to hate their father's assassins. Buddhists believe that if you hurt people, even for revenge, you will suffer in your next life. This is the law of karma: each person must control his or her own ignorance, hatred, and desire, or suffer the consequences in this life or the next.

After Aung San's death, Daw Khin Kyi was appointed director of social welfare in Burma's independent government, led by prime minister U Nu, Aung San's colleague. Without a parent at home during the day, Suu Kyi and her brothers were cared for by aunts, uncles, older cousins, and even some of her father's devoted friends and military colleagues. There was no shortage of adults to influence and guide Suu Kyi.

Because of her husband's love of literature, Daw Khin Kyi promoted reading at home. Even though she was not a great reader herself, she took her children to the library every two weeks. But when Suu Kyi was young, she would rather listen to stories than read them herself. "My great aunt, my grandfather's younger sister, was always telling stories from the *Jataka* [tales of the early lives of the Buddha]. She knew the whole story of the Buddha's life. Her knowledge of Buddhism was really very, very broad, and she taught us a lot, especially me because she felt closer to me because I was a girl. I learned about Buddhism the easy way."

Like most Buddhists, Suu Kyi's family had a small altar at home. There they made offerings of fresh water, flowers, fruit, and incense every morning.

Suu Kyi also visited Rangoon's famous Shwedagon Pagoda, the biggest Buddhist temple of its kind in the world. She would climb the pagoda's long staircase to the central pagoda and stand in awe of its multispired roofs, golden statues, and intricate wood carvings.

Daw Khin Kyi was quite strict with her children. She

The Shwedagon Pagoda is the central place of worship for Buddhists in Burma.

brought them up to respect elders and to live by traditional Burmese values: modesty, hospitality, consideration, and generosity. Daw Khin Kyi was so principled and serious that some of her nieces and nephews were afraid of her. According to Daw Than E, "Daw Khin Kyi impressed upon the children their obligations to Burmese social and moral values and brought them up in the Buddhist faith."

Suu Kyi learned from her mother's example and was dutiful and polite, especially in the company of adults.

At age six, Suu Kyi liked to play with her cousins and brothers.

She carried herself with silent confidence, her back a straight line. She had soft dark eyes and rounded lips, but her furled eyebrows hinted at internal intensity. When she was smiling and relaxed, her face seemed to give off light. Their family friend, Daw Than E, wrote about the young girl's beauty and respectful behavior: "Suu, in my view, is an exemplar of what we Burmese regard as seemly, in matters of dress, comportment, conduct and bearing, in public and private."

Despite her mother's insistent demand for proper conduct, Aung San Suu Kyi knew her mother was a very warm person—the most important person in her early life. According to Suu Kyi, they were close in a typically Burmese way: "I had a very Burmese relationship with her, which means that mothers don't really discuss personal problems with their children. Parents don't do that, in a Burmese context. There is a certain reserve between the generations. Mothers of my mother's generation just don't have heart-to-heart talks with their daughters." Because of this reserve between mother and daughter, Suu Kyi learned to hold her emotions within herself, to have strict self-control.

Although Suu Kyi had to keep her feelings in check, she was still an ordinary child who liked to play with the dolls that were given to her by friends and family. She also played with her brothers, especially Aung San Lin, and her cousins who lived nearby.

Schoolmates thought of Suu Kyi as a tomboy. Both in school and at home, she liked to wear clunky shoes, keep her hair in two long braids, and play games often reserved for boys. When schoolboys teased her, she stood up to them.

Suu Kyi's brother Aung San Lin was an adventurous, intelligent boy who loved to play with his sister. They also shared a bedroom. One day when Suu Kyi was seven and a half, after one of their games at the edge of an ornamental lake near their house, Aung San Lin suddenly drowned. "He dropped his little toy gun at the edge of the lake and went back to get it. His sandal got dislodged in mud, and he ran back and gave me the gun. Then he went back for his sandal, and he never came back."

Her brother's death was extremely hard for Suu Kyi. She missed him deeply. "I think in some way the death of my second brother affected me more than my father's death."

Daw Khin Kyi, with Aung San U and Suu Kyi

When she was told her son had drowned, Daw Khin Kyi again appeared stoic. She was at her office, and she finished her work before she went home. Her social duty came before her personal life.

After Aung San Lin's death, the family moved from their home into a new house on Inya Lake, not far from Rangoon University. There, family life was just as busy as before, and Suu Kyi continued to meet people of many different backgrounds, religions, and political views. Although she was raised a Buddhist, her maternal grandfather, who was a Christian, taught her to be open-minded about faith. Suu Kyi read the Bible to him in Burmese. She learned an acceptance of all religions: "I'm all for a broadminded attitude. People of all different religions should be given the opportunity to pursue good in their own way. I assume that is what religion is all about. Religion is about increasing peace and harmony in the world. Everyone should be given a chance to create peace and harmony in their own way."

Aung San Suu Kyi had one strong childhood fear. "I used to be terribly frightened of the dark. I could not bear to go into a dark room by myself. I think I was afraid of ghosts because the Burmese are very fond of ghost stories."

When Suu Kyi was about twelve years old, she planned a way to face her fear of the dark. Every evening, Daw Khin Kyi made hot milk for her children to drink. Suu Kyi did not like her milk hot, so she left it downstairs until it cooled off. Later in the evening, after everyone was upstairs, she would go downstairs by herself to drink her milk. She had decided to use this time to get used to wandering around the rooms in the dark. "The first few days my heart would go 'thump, thump, thump', but after five or six days I got quite used to it."

In the late 1950s, Suu Kyi attended the Methodist English High School. The school accepted most of its twelve hundred students from prominent Buddhist Burmese families, along with Indian and Chinese children. Although the instruction at this school had a Christian orientation and was based on a traditional British educational model, many classes were taught in Burmese, and Buddhist students were not made to convert to Christianity. Students listened to lectures and learned subjects by repetition. They had no cooperative, hands-on learning, nor extracurricular activities.

> I USED TO BE TERRIBLY FRIGHTENED OF THE DARK. I COULD NOT BEAR TO GO INTO A DARK ROOM BY MYSELF.

According to her classmates, Suu Kyi was not treated in any special way at school for being Aung San's daughter. She was, however, noticed for her intelligence and her talent for languages. She was at the top of her class and was also considered fair and self-reliant.

In 1959 an American science teacher, Bob Fuller, came to teach at the school. He thought that the American school model was too easy, and he hoped to discover better standards at this British missionary school. After a short time at the school, he realized that students needed extracurricular activities to help them expand their

Students from all over Burma gather in front of the Methodist English High School before taking national exams.

learning environment. Fuller organized a science club and coordinated a national science competition. He also taught a class on morals in which he helped students broaden their views and increase their tolerance of human differences. Suu Kyi said her morals class made an impression on her and helped her understand people of different backgrounds: "If there is understanding then you don't have to solve your problems through violence; you can solve them by just talking it over. If there was understanding, in fact, there would be few problems."

Smugglers, laden with goods, cross a river as they travel from Thailand into Burma.

CHAPTER FOUR

LESSONS FROM A LARGER WORLD

BURMA HAD BECOME AN INDEPENDENT COUNTRY in 1948—the year after Suu Kyi's father was assassinated. The government was then led by the prime minister, U Nu. Because the country had suffered under Japanese occupation during World War II, the new government inherited overwhelming economic and social problems. At the same time, ethnic and political groups throughout the country argued with each other. Some groups isolated and armed themselves. Others aligned themselves with foreign armies. Communists operated in the hill country. Some ethnic groups rebelled. And Chinese nationalists moved into Burma as they tried to escape communist China's People's Liberation Army.

By 1953, Chinese nationalists took over parts of the Shan State in Burma. There they created an opium smuggling operation that spilled over into Laos and Thailand. This area became known as the "Golden Triangle," the largest supplier of illegal heroin in the world. Lacking natural resources and cash crops, some of the ethnic groups in Burma also got involved in producing opium.

Although Burma experienced economic crises in the late 1940s and 1950s, and it relied upon loans from Japan, the United States, the World Bank, and communist countries, some Burmese thought of this time as one of liberty and openness. People could have foreign friends, operate private businesses, travel and trade abroad, and talk openly about personal views.

In 1960, Daw Khin Kyi was appointed Burma's ambassador to India. At first Aung San Suu Kyi did not want to move to India and leave her best friends at home. After

Daw Khin Kyi (right) *is installed as Burma's ambassador to India.*

she and her mother moved into their New Delhi house, however, Suu Kyi quickly adjusted and made new friends. Her older brother, Aung San U, went off to college in England to study electrical engineering and returned to Asia only on vacations.

In New Delhi, Suu Kyi was busy with schoolwork from the Convent of Jesus and Mary, or with lessons and entertaining. She learned to play the piano, and she took a class in Japanese flower arrangement. She also took riding lessons during which she met diplomats, Indian officials, and the sons of Indira Gandhi, Rajiv and Sanjay.

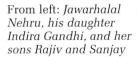

From left: *Jawarhalal Nehru, his daughter Indira Gandhi, and her sons Rajiv and Sanjay*

Rajiv and Sanjay's grandfather, Jawarhalal Nehru, was the prime minister of India. Suu Kyi's father had met and discussed politics with Nehru on several occasions, so Nehru was not a stranger to Aung San's family.

During Suu Kyi's teenage years in India, she became passionate about reading. Many guests who visited the New Delhi house recommended books that inspired Suu Kyi and helped her form her political philosophy. One of Aung San's colleagues, a Burmese journalist named U Ohn, gave Suu Kyi many books and wrote out long lists of other books for her to read. Suu Kyi read Greek mythology, English and Burmese literature, and political philosophy. All this reading made her think about becoming a writer.

Suu Kyi loved reading the works of Mohandas Gandhi. In the 1940s, Gandhi—later known as *Mahatma,* which means "Great Soul"—helped bring India to its independence from Britain. He promoted nonviolence and peaceful civil disobedience, eventually forcing the British government to release its control of India. Even at an early age, Suu Kyi understood the power of nonviolent negotiation and compromise.

In New Delhi, Suu Kyi and her mother were active participants in a community of people from all over the world. With the help of other Buddhists in India, Daw Khin Kyi restored a Buddhist center in a suburb of New Delhi. With this restoration, mother and daughter, and many other Buddhists, had a place for meditation and ceremony.

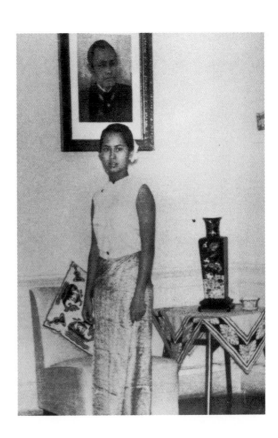

Suu Kyi stands under a portrait of her father at home in New Delhi.

Daw Khin Kyi welcomed many guests to her home, Burma's embassy in New Delhi. Buddhist monks from Burma, Thailand, and Cambodia called on her, and she hosted parties for other political leaders. Alert, polite, and serious, Suu Kyi took part in many of these events. As a teenager, Suu Kyi was usually quiet and correct, by Burmese standards. For the most part, she remained in the background when her mother entertained.

Harold O'Brien, a British journalist who visited Daw Khin Kyi's house in New Delhi, described mother and daughter: "Her mother's clothes matched perfectly. Her hair was done up perfectly with a flower in the bun. She let you talk, and she laughed gently, and then she made biting remarks. Suu arrived, and I remember being struck by how she plunged into the conversation about politics. She was seventeen or eighteen, and she was already a commanding person. . . . Her mother was a bit more relaxed than Suu. You could have a good chuckle with her. Suu was more correct."

After high school, Suu Kyi studied political science at Delhi University for two years. During this time, Burma underwent dramatic political changes. U Nu had done what he could to keep the country together, but rebellious minority groups were too strong for his government. From October 1958 until February 1960, U Nu's power was usurped. Ne Win stepped in to hold the country in control. He was the military officer once applauded for his participation with the Thirty Comrades in the fight against the British—the man Suu Kyi's father had not liked.

In February 1960, Ne Win called for national elections to reinstate a civilian government, and U Nu won by a large majority. U Nu reorganized his party, but despite his popularity and his efforts to strengthen democracy in Burma, he still could not end the infighting and rebellion. U Nu called a meeting of all minority leaders to find a solution to each group's problems—but before he could implement any solution, he was challenged by Ne Win. This time Ne Win planned to keep the power.

Ne Win used the army to support himself. On March 2, 1962, he dissolved the parliament, threw out the constitution that had been drawn up by Aung San and the executive committee, and arrested Burma's political leaders, including U Nu. Ne Win then formed an advisory board, the Revolutionary Council, with his military colleagues. Ne Win explained that he had seized power because he feared U Nu would allow the Shan State to secede from Burma. More importantly, the constitutional

Ne Win (right) meets with Nehru during a trip to India.

government had failed to transform the promise of socialism into reality.

On April 30, 1962, Ne Win began to inflict even more
drastic changes on Burma. He announced his plan for the
new "Burmese Way to Socialism." Because none of the
political parties in Burma would support the Revolutionary Council, the council formed its own party called the
Burma Socialist Programme Party (BSPP). Its member-
ship was made up mostly of men in the military. The
BSPP tried to gain support of ordinary citizens through
community instruction and propaganda, but it could not

The presence of the Burmese army is felt all over Rangoon.

control civil wars in Burma. Many Buddhist students and monks protested against the new government, but they were suppressed by military force.

In addition, Ne Win declared that Burma was closed to the West. Western foreigners were forced to leave. The government took over banks, industry, education, and communication systems in Burma. The military was not prepared to manage the production and distribution of products that had formerly been controlled by the private sector, so there were shortages of food, fuel, and basic necessities. A black market was immediately formed to bring goods to the people of Burma.

Throughout this period of political turmoil in Burma, Aung San Suu Kyi lived in India. She did not get involved in activities that either supported or rejected Ne Win's military government, but she kept an eye on Burma's problems. Although some people believed that Suu Kyi had forgotten her country while she lived abroad, those who knew her well understood the depth of Suu Kyi's continued devotion to Burma.

> IF I WERE TO ENGAGE IN ANY POLITICAL MOVEMENT I WOULD DO SO FROM WITHIN THE COUNTRY.

Suu Kyi wrote about her concern for Burma during her years away: "If I were to engage in any political movement I would do so from within the country. . . . It was not difficult to recognize that the nation was inexorably deteriorating under the government of the BSPP. But I could not see any signs of a popular opposition movement which I could support wholeheartedly."

Suu Kyi attended Oxford University in Oxford, England.

■

CHAPTER FIVE

SHARPENING A POLITICAL MIND

IN 1964, AFTER PREPARING HERSELF FOR AN education abroad, Suu Kyi went off to Oxford University in England. When Suu Kyi arrived in England, Sir Paul Gore-Booth and his wife Patricia opened their London house to her. Suu Kyi had gotten to know their family when Sir Paul had been ambassador to Burma and, later, high commissioner in New Delhi. The Gore-Booths had twin sons and two daughters, and they welcomed Suu Kyi into their family.

At this London home, Suu Kyi was introduced to many of her hosts' friends and political colleagues. She was curious about these guests. She watched their behavior and listened to their language. Because of her intelligence and beauty, many people were curious about her, too.

Among the people that Suu Kyi met at the Gore-Booth home were Michael and Anthony Aris, another set of twins. Patricia Gore-Booth watched as Michael Aris, a student of Tibetan studies, fell in love with Suu Kyi right away. Mrs. Gore-Booth doubted that Suu Kyi would ever consider having a romance with a Westerner. Many Burmese people didn't accept interracial marriages. Burmese friends and relatives would be strongly against a marriage of Aung San's daughter to a Western man.

After Aung San Suu Kyi and Michael Aris met, they saw each other regularly at the Gore-Booth's house or at Michael's home. Michael also traveled the fifty-six miles from London to Oxford to visit Suu Kyi.

Michael Aris and Aung San Suu Kyi

At Oxford University, Suu Kyi was accepted into the program of politics, philosophy, and economics. She would have preferred to study English literature or forestry, but she was not accepted into those degree programs. She did realize that by learning about economics, she might, one day, be useful to her developing country.

Suu Kyi arrived at Oxford and immediately stood out because of her formal appearance, her strong ideals, and her innocence. She wore a starched cotton shirt and a traditional Burmese *longyi*—an ankle-length, wrapped skirt. She looked very proper next to classmates dressed in the loose, ragged clothes worn by many students in England in the 1960s. Suu Kyi was considered a "goody-goody." She did her work, starched her Burmese cotton blouses in the dormitory basement, and followed university rules.

After her second year, however, she was curious to imitate her friends. For the first time, she bought herself some white jeans and learned to ride a bicycle. In the bathroom at college, she tried alcohol for the first time, and she hated it.

Most of Suu's dormitory friends talked about their boyfriends. The young women tried to look cool and mature, even when they weren't. They acted loose about love affairs and denounced traditional relationships as old-fashioned. Suu Kyi, on the other hand, told her friends she would not have sex with anyone but her husband. Her friends laughed at her, but Suu Kyi stayed true to herself.

Eventually, Suu Kyi tried one of her friends' tricks. Suu

Kyi went out on a date and snuck back into the dorm—
after curfew. This practice was called "climbing in," and
students who did it were seen as daring. Suu Kyi wasn't
going to be considered completely prudish forever, even
if she refused to compromise her highly principled
manners.

After earning a degree from Oxford University in 1967,
Suu Kyi worked as a research assistant for Professor
Hugh Tinker in the political science department at the
School of Oriental and African Studies at London Uni-
versity. She also taught at an English preparatory school
for boys.

In 1969, Suu Kyi moved to New York City, where she
lived with Daw Than E, who was working for the United
Nations (UN). Suu Kyi had planned to start postgraduate
studies at New York University, but was persuaded to ap-
ply for a job at the UN first. After a long interview
process, Suu Kyi was hired. She worked in a few different offices until she was finally placed on the Advisory
Committee on Administrative and Budgetary Questions.
The members of this committee oversaw the budgets and
programs of all the branches and special departments in
the UN. According to Daw Than E, "It was extremely
hard work, but most interesting for its close examination
of the financial implications of all UN activities, and for
its members, people with exceptional minds. Suu came
to know them well."

In addition to her job at the UN, Suu Kyi volunteered
many hours each week at Belleview, part of New York

Suu Kyi worked at the United Nations in New York.

Hospital. Belleview cared for some of the most mentally distraught and physically ill people in the city. Volunteers were always needed for special programs and companionship for the patients. Suu Kyi saw great value in helping poor, desperate people.

During Suu Kyi's years in New York City, she relaxed and learned about American culture by going to concerts, restaurants, and movies. She and Daw Than E spent a good deal of time with the UN secretary-general, a

The UN secretary-general, U Thant

Burmese man named U Thant, who held parties at his house overlooking the Hudson River. There Suu Kyi ate delicious Burmese food and chatted with Burmese friends.

At other times, the two visited Soe Tin, Burma's ambassador to the UN. He invited many Burmese guests to his house to celebrate Burmese holidays. He and his wife were jovial and open-minded, and they encouraged all types of conversations, including political debates, which most Burmese usually avoided because of government restrictions in Burma. People had no freedom to criticize the government.

One time, Suu Kyi and Daw Than E were invited to Soe Tin's house because some members of a Burmese delegation to the UN wanted to meet them. Daw Than E suspected something unusual about this meeting, but she did not know what. After the women arrived and were seated next to the Burmese delegates, the senior Burmese official began to speak to Suu Kyi. He reprimanded her for holding a diplomatic passport, which she should have given up because her mother was no longer ambassador to India. A diplomatic passport provided Suu Kyi with travel and employment privileges, but the Burmese government wanted her to have the status and passport of an ordinary citizen. The Burmese official also had questions about her work at the UN.

Despite the man's aggressive manner, Suu Kyi remained calm and collected in her response. She spoke quietly and with respect. She told him that she had applied for a new passport in London months ago. She had no idea why it had not arrived. She also explained that she was in New York to study and had had to find a job to cover living expenses. She told the Burmese officials she could not give up her current passport, which she needed to live in the United States and work at the UN, until her new one arrived. The ambassador from London validated Suu Kyi's claim that she had applied in London. He too had had no response from Rangoon. Everyone in the room knew that the problem had originated in Burma. Since the military takeover of the country in 1962, bureaucratic chaos was common. After listening to Suu Kyi, the chief delegate excused himself, and the matter was dropped. Suu Kyi had stood up to a member of Burma's military regime, and she had remained strong and calm.

Michael Aris and Aung San Suu Kyi were married in 1972.

BETWEEN WORK AND FAMILY

IN 1971, WHILE SUU KYI WAS WORKING IN NEW York City, she wrote 187 letters to Michael Aris. He was more than seven thousand miles away, working as tutor to the royal family in Bhutan, a Himalayan country next to Tibet and Nepal.

Suu Kyi wrote that she was concerned her family and the Burmese people might misunderstand her relationship with a foreigner. Many Burmese people believed that anyone who married a foreigner rejected their roots and culture. Although Suu Kyi knew she was not rejecting her family or country, she could be seen as causing her family embarrassment in society. She spent a long period considering marriage to Michael Aris.

Burma's former ambassador to Britain, Chit Myaing, explained: "The Burmese people would not like the daughter of Aung San marrying a foreigner. I knew that if I attended the wedding, I would be fired that day."

Suu Kyi wrote to Michael about her need to return to Burma if the Burmese people ever needed her. Although Suu Kyi did not plan to have a career in politics, she did imagine herself working for her country. She thought she might some day organize a public library system in Burma and a scholarship program for Burmese students. She had studied economics at Oxford with the idea that she might offer her experience and understanding to her country.

In a letter, Suu Kyi asked Michael to promise to allow her to help Burma, if need be.

> I only ask one thing, that should my people need me, you would help me to do my duty by them.
>
> Would you mind very much should such a situation ever arise? How probable it is I do not know, but the possibility is there.
>
> Sometimes I am beset by fears that circumstances and national considerations might tear us apart just when we are so happy in each other that separation would be a torment. And yet such fears are so futile and inconsequential: if we love and cherish each other as much as we can while we can, I am sure that love and compassion will triumph in the end.

Michael promised.

In 1971, Suu Kyi took a trip to Burma. On her way back to New York, she visited Michael in Bhutan. He showed her the mountains and wooded valleys of western Bhutan.

By the time Suu Kyi returned to the United States, she and Michael had become engaged. On New Year's day in 1972, the two were married in a Buddhist ceremony at the Gore-Booth's house in London.

Even young Burmese realized how difficult Suu Kyi's decision to marry Michael must have been. One student commented: "Her marriage to Aris, no doubt in my mind, must have torn her apart, regardless of how strong and stubborn she may be. (We as an ethnic group, still don't want to accept interracial/religious marriages, and it's the end of the 20th century.)"

> I ONLY ASK ONE THING, THAT SHOULD MY PEOPLE NEED ME, YOU WOULD HELP ME TO DO MY DUTY BY THEM. . . . HOW PROBABLE IT IS I DO NOT KNOW, BUT THE POSSIBILITY IS THERE.

Suu Kyi quit her job in New York and went back to Bhutan with Michael. Because of her experience at the UN, she was hired by the Bhutanese Foreign Ministry to advise the office on UN policy. In addition to this work, Suu Kyi volunteered to teach English to the Royal Bhutan Bodyguards in a schoolhouse behind the couple's home in Thimphu, Bhutan's capital. As a wedding present from the king's chamberlain, the couple received a Himalayan terrier named Puppy. The little dog, living and traveling with the family, made Suu Kyi very happy.

As she participated in a traditional Asian society that was different from her own, Suu Kyi learned about the social and educational problems that went along with the richness of Bhutan's culture. She made many friends in this country of little more than one million inhabitants.

These friends—government officers, monks, scholars, ordinary villagers, and members of the royal family—all remained devoted to her long after she left their country.

The young couple stayed in Bhutan for two years. Then, in 1973, they returned to England for Michael's doctoral studies. They moved into a nutshell of an apartment in London, and there they started a family. On April 12, 1973, Suu Kyi gave birth to their first son, Alexander. She quickly became a devoted, kind mother.

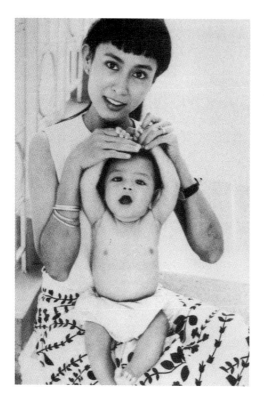

Suu Kyi holds her son, Alexander.

In 1976 the small family moved to Oxford. Michael received a junior fellowship at St. John's College. Suu Kyi was busy running a household, caring for Alexander, receiving guests, and reading. Then on September 24, 1977, the couple had a second son, whom they named Kim.

Suu Kyi's household was "elegant and calm." She knew how to shop economically, sew clothes for herself and her family, and cook Burmese, English, French, and Chinese food. Suu Kyi was crazy about reading—she enjoyed biographies, poetry, fiction, and travel literature. She loved listening to music, playing the piano, and taking walks. When the family had vacation time, they made trips to Switzerland, Germany, Scotland, India, Nepal, Thailand, and Japan. They also made frequent visits to Burma to visit Daw Khin Kyi. Suu Kyi often suffered from motion sickness in cars and planes, but it never hindered her pleasure in travel.

Even when the nursery had to double as a guest room and the family budget limited activities, Suu Kyi and Michael managed with good spirits. They were always hospitable to their many visitors from all over the world, and they provided a loving, secure life for their sons.

A friend of Suu Kyi's from Oxford believed that, beneath a tranquil surface, Suu Kyi was "impatient for new challenges." Other friends wondered if home life was enough to satisfy Suu Kyi, a woman of such great intellect. Even Michael said she was "basically dissatisfied with her life because she couldn't do something for her country."

But Suu Kyi said, "I was ordinarily happy. I was happy. I mean we all had our ups and downs, of course. We moved house a great deal because of Michael's work. We traveled a lot. But, life in Oxford is easy. It's very calm, far calmer than life in a capital city like Rangoon."

In addition to handling her household, Suu Kyi kept herself intellectually stimulated. She surrounded herself with Burmese, English, and French literature. From 1975 until 1977, she worked in the Bodleian Library at Oxford University, cataloging Burmese books.

Suu Kyi's sons, Alexander and Kim, were brought up in the academic and international environment created

From left: *Suu Kyi, Kim, Michael, and Alexander celebrate Christmas at Oxford in 1984.*

by Michael and Suu Kyi. Both boys attended the Dragon School in Oxford. Kim shared his mother's love of music and learned to play guitar, whereas Alexander became interested in sports and philosophy.

Suu Kyi turned her efforts to writing a biography of her father. She began research of his life that took her to several countries: Burma, England, India, and Japan. She taught herself Japanese, and then she and Kim spent a year in Kyoto. Michael stayed in England with Alexander and continued his own research.

In Kyoto, Suu Kyi had the first opportunity to do her own research since the birth of her sons. As she consulted documents that pertained to her father's activities with the Japanese and the role of the Japanese in the Burmese army, she immersed herself in the Japanese world of sophisticated scholarship. Suu Kyi appreciated Japanese culture—the arts and literature, the attention to society's spiritual development, and the cuisine.

Because Suu Kyi had a "rare gift for real friendship," she was well received in Japan. That year, she and Kim made many lifelong friends.

The following year, in 1987, the entire family moved to Simla, in northern India. Both Suu Kyi and Michael did research at the Indian Institute of Advanced Study. Simla had been the summer capital when the British ruled India. When the heat on the Indian plains climbed over one hundred degrees Fahrenheit, the British, and later the Indian leaders, traveled north to the British-style lodges built on mountainsides above eight thousand feet.

Before she joined her family in Simla, Suu Kyi spent a month in London with her mother. Daw Khin Kyi needed a cataract operation and wanted it done in England where the medical system was modern and Suu Kyi could easily care for her.

When Suu Kyi reached Simla, she was introduced to the many Indian and foreign scholars who were guests of the institute. The institute was housed in the Viceregal Lodge—the summer offices of the viceroy, or governor-general, of India when it was a British colony. Michael, Suu Kyi, and the boys occupied the turret of the Viceregal Lodge. From there they had a glorious view of the snowcapped Himalayan peaks.

Suu Kyi and her family, like the other scholars and families, ate breakfasts and dinners in the grand dining room, where the names of the viceroys were inscribed above the rich dark wood paneling. For other meals, the family cooked in a makeshift kitchen without refrigeration. They often served dinners to some of the other scholars, offering such simple foods as mashed potatoes, eggs, cheese, and pancakes.

As the family settled into life at the institute, ten-year-old Kim went to a local elementary school and fourteen-year-old Alexander studied by himself during the day, until about four-thirty in the afternoon. Michael and Suu Kyi retreated into books and documents. When the day's study was over, Suu Kyi and her family often relaxed with other scholars at the institute.

One American family, the Clymers, had two children

Michael and Suu Kyi shared one of the huge turret rooms in the Viceregal Lodge for their study.

the same ages as Alexander and Kim. Aron Clymer and Alexander often played Monopoly, shared books, and tossed toy airplanes and Frisbees on the institute grounds, while Megan Clymer and Kim acted out fantastical tales and played in a makeshift tent.

The Clymers and other institute scholars noticed that Suu Kyi, Michael, and the boys were a close and loving family. Both parents showed great concern and patience with their sons. And both Michael and Suu Kyi often called each other "darling" or "sweetheart." They were open about their affection and admiration for each other.

Michael and Suu Kyi with their friend Kyaw Win in Simla, India

"He loved her deeply. She loved him deeply. They were a very solid couple that was operating easily together on well-worn tracks," said an American friend. "They did everything in a reasonable order. They'd all sit down and have breakfast. And, there was tea at regular times. The relationship was one of complete equality between husband and wife who loved each other dearly."

Daw Khin Kyi attends the Buddhist initiation ceremony of her grandsons, Alexander and Kim, in 1987.

One day, not long after the Clymers and Suu Kyi arrived at the institute, the local Indian police came to visit Michael, Kenton Clymer, and some other scholars. The police had been informed that these foreigners were carrying out espionage at the institute and were pretending to be scholars. The police ordered an investigation, and they demanded to see the passports and visas of the scholars. They even questioned Michael about his telescope that was turned in the direction of a sensitive Indian military position. Everyone knew Michael used the telescope to look at stars, not the ground. The scholars had no idea why the police were suspicious.

In early June, Indian newspapers began to publish articles about the foreign spies in Simla, which caused the scholars some worry. While the police continued to question everything the scholars did, Suu Kyi, Michael, and Kenton and Marlee Clymer got together and discussed the situation.

Suu Kyi was ignited by this malicious accusation. She spent hours trying to figure out who had called the police. Within a short time, Suu Kyi had theories about who was making the trouble. Some of the group assumed that Indian scholars were trying to get rid of the foreigners. Others believed that someone wanted to turn the institute into a five-star hotel. Still others guessed that some Indian scholars were just trying to get back at the institute director, who was not well liked. Suu Kyi became engaged in defense of the foreign scholars.

"She came alive," said Marlee Clymer. "She exudes power. I think she loves a good fight."

"She was very striking, very forceful," Kenton Clymer added. "She showed herself to be very much a leader. She was not shy about expressing her opinions."

Another American scholar thought this event showed Suu Kyi's innate political wisdom. "She had a fierce political intelligence. There was something almost made of steel about her. I think it comes from her father, that it's inherited. Of course I didn't know him. Whatever it was that made her father what he was, she has."

The director of the institute was away when the spy story erupted. As soon as the director returned to Simla,

Suu Kyi, at the Viceregal Lodge

she looked into the matter. Suddenly, the police investigation died down, and nothing came of it. It was a situation, however, in which Suu Kyi's determination and sense of justice propelled her to action.

During a food shortage in Burma, even rice is sold on the black market.

STUDENTS AT THE FRONT

IN 1987, WHILE SUU KYI, MICHAEL, AND THE BOYS were in India, Burma's quality of life continued to spiral downward under Ne Win's government. The economy was dismal. Ever since Ne Win had taken control of Burma's government twenty-five years before, his policies had provoked anger and protest from the Burmese people. Inflation was so great that ordinary citizens could hardly afford rice—the main food in their diet. Education, health care, and public services, such as indoor plumbing and phone service, were luxuries only rich families could afford. And most of the rich were those who had connections to the government.

On December 11, 1987, Burma was granted the status of Least Developed Country (LDC) by the United Nations. Burma's per capita income was less than two hundred dollars per year. The people were strongly oppressed. If they protested the injustice, however, they were arrested and often tortured. Criticizing the government was against the law.

Ne Win silenced anyone who questioned his power, even his own protégés if they became too popular. He developed a secret police force, which he used to uncover dissension of any kind. He created interrogation centers where citizens were questioned and tortured. "Total submission was required to survive in the new Burma that the military was creating: a Burma built not on trust and consensus, but under dictatorial rule by one man alone."

In the late 1980s, Ne Win appointed a new chief of intelligence—a man named Khin Nyunt, who had been a petty commander in the army. In 1988, Khin Nyunt faced Burma's nationwide demonstrations, and he planned to suppress the people. By then, Suu Kyi and her family had moved back to Oxford where life was steady and calm.

A phone call on March 31 broke the family's quiet. "It was a quiet evening in Oxford like many others the last day of March 1988," Michael said. "Our sons were already in bed and we were reading when the telephone rang. Suu picked up the phone to learn that her mother had suffered a severe stroke. She put the phone down and at once started to pack. I had a premonition that our lives would change forever. Two days later Suu was many thousands of miles away at her mother's bedside in Rangoon."

In Rangoon, Suu Kyi stayed in the Rangoon General Hospital with her mother. After three months, Suu Kyi and the doctors realized that Daw Khin Kyi was not getting better. She was released to die quietly in her own home. Suu Kyi set up a bedroom in the downstairs study of her childhood home on Inya Lake, and there she kept the atmosphere loving and calm for her mother. At the next school break, Alexander and Kim joined Suu Kyi in Rangoon.

Outside Suu Kyi's house, life was not so calm.

The military and riot police had been using drastic force whenever they faced community resistance. On March 12, 1988, a brawl had broken out between students from the Rangoon Institute of Technology and drunken locals at a small tea shop near the institute. The reason for the argument was not clear, but there were at least three theories. Some say the fight was over a gambling debt. Others say it was political. Most people, however, say the students and locals fought over what type of music to play on the shop's tape player. One of the students, Win Myint, was stabbed with a knife, and his classmates reported the injury to the police. The locals who hurt the student were arrested but released the next day. One of the locals was the son of a member of the ruling party, the Burma Socialist Programme Party (BSPP), so he and his companions were not kept in jail.

On March 13, when the students discovered that the locals had gone free, they were furious and demanded justice. The government would not listen to the students' protest. Instead it sent out the riot police armed with clubs and automatic rifles. Students, who were fed up with the government's mismanagement of education and the lack of job prospects after college, didn't want to take any more governmental abuse. They began to throw rocks at the riot police—then the troops shot back. In an instant, students scattered, but many of them were hit by bullets. One young man, Maung Phone Maw, was hit and later died. At least two others, chained to their beds in the hospital and kept under armed guard, died from festering wounds or blood loss.

This tea shop brawl, and the death of Maung Phone Maw, contributed to the start of a great resistance move-

Burmese people begin to demonstrate against the military government.

ment. The Burmese people were tired of watching the military take every privilege while they suffered. The student marches started nationwide demonstrations.

On March 16, a small group of students from the Rangoon Institute of Technology joined students from the nearby Rangoon University on the university campus. They marched together from the campus, up Prome Road, by Inya Lake, toward the institute.

As the students marched, they were blocked by military forces at the edge of Inya Lake. They could not move forward into the military nor backward into the riot police forces that cut off the road from the other end. The students tried to negotiate with the military officer in front, but he declared he had orders not to let students pass. None of the soldiers would speak to the students. The riot police threw tear gas into the crowd, yanked jewelry off female students, beat students with clubs, then threw them into trucks.

As students began screaming and trying to escape, the military started shooting. Many of the young people ran toward the White Bridge over Inya Lake and were forced into the water. Some students who could not swim drowned in the lake. Others were held underwater by soldiers until they died. Many more, especially women, were beaten severely. So many students were beaten or died at the White Bridge that its name was changed forever. Although the government denies any violence on this day, March 16 became "Red Bridge Day."

One student, Khin Ohmar, who escaped behind the

gates of a private residence, said she saw students being beaten by the riot police. She also said that her boyfriend, Zaw Zaw, "was beaten and dragged. He was arrested that day with other friends. He was in jail for four months, not released until July 7th when students demanded the release of their jailed friends. . . . They were all expelled from school and put on a black list"—a list of students who dared to oppose the government.

Zaw Zaw suffered terribly in prison. He was beaten and tortured and given nothing but rancid food. He, along with many other political prisoners, developed a severe skin rash from eating bad fish paste. They had nothing to drink but lead-poisoned water. Zaw Zaw's worst days were spent in an isolation cell. "I was scared and I was screaming to get out. The second day I tried to meditate to calm down and remember Buddhist prayers. It was hard to concentrate and control myself. I thought I'd go crazy."

On March 18, many citizens joined students in a demonstration in central Rangoon near the Sule Pagoda. The riot police and the military again used brutal force. The screaming and bloodshed horrified onlookers who hid in buildings, but the demonstrators were not defeated. Those who were not arrested banded together. Others, who were caught by the police, suffered terribly.

One high school student, Nyi Nyi Aung, participated in the March 18 protests because he wanted the public to know what the riot police had done to university students since March 13. He spoke to the crowds until a tear

Burmese troops confront protesters in central Rangoon.

gas canister hit his leg, causing him to be dizzy and temporarily blinded. He tried to go home, but all the roads were blocked by the riot police. Finally, after hiding out in a monastery in the city, Nyi Nyi started home. He was arrested by the police and thrown into a truck crowded with nearly eighty other people. Nobody could easily stand or sit in the small truck, and people began to suffocate. After almost five hours in the truck, the arrested people were escorted into jails. Some had already died and were lying in pools of sweat, blood, urine, and excrement in the truck.

For the next month, while Nyi Nyi suffered the hardship of prison, his family did not know where he was. In order to earn his freedom, he denied participating in the riots. He told nobody the truth. He was tortured anyway.

"I didn't trust anybody in jail," he said. "I slept on the bare floor. I had no blanket, pillow, or mattress. Even sick students were without blankets and got no medical care. We ate watery soup that had dirt and stones in it, and a little rice and vegetables two times a day. We all drank water from one cup. . . . After one month, the police made me sign papers that I could not read, and then they released me."

In the chaos, General Ne Win suddenly announced he was retiring as leader. In his place, he picked a man named Sein Lwin who had been loyal to him. General Sein Lwin was notorious for leading army attacks on students in 1962 and during the 1970s. He was nicknamed "the Butcher of Rangoon."

Nobody actually believed that Ne Win had relinquished all power. They guessed he secretly ran the government from his residence on Inya Lake. In Ne Win's televised resignation speech, he warned the people of Burma that if there were any more demonstrations, the army would not fire warning shots. It would shoot to kill.

Ne Win meant what he said. The people, however, wanted to fight for justice. Suu Kyi—who was spending her days caring for her mother—was asked to help mediate between the military government and the students. Former politicians, as well as army officials, had many discussions with her. At the same time, monks, doctors, lawyers, businesspeople, artists, writers, housewives, farmers, children, and laborers joined the student movement and planned a strike. Before arranging an important activity such as this, they needed to consult an astrologer for the most auspicious, or favorable, date. The astrologer told them that August 8, 1988—8/8/88—was the most auspicious.

At 8:08, the morning of August 8, hundreds of thousands of people came out into the main streets of Rangoon. One witness standing on a hotel balcony downtown described the demonstration: "Then the first marchers arrived. I saw them coming in a massive column across the railway bridge on Sule Pagoda Road with flags and banners, heading for the city center. There were thousands of them, clenching their fists and chanting antigovernment slogans. People came out of their houses, applauding and cheering the demonstrators on."

On August 8, 1988, hundreds of thousands of Burmese march down
the streets of Rangoon.

Even some of the police join the pro-democracy demonstrators.

The demonstration lasted all day. The people thought that Ne Win had backed down, but they were wrong. At about eleven-thirty at night, trucks full of armed soldiers moved out from behind City Hall. Instead of scattering, the demonstrators sang Burma's national anthem. Then suddenly, the calm was shattered. "Two pistol shots rang out—and then the sound of machine-gun fire reverberated in the dark between the old, colonial buildings of central Rangoon. People fell in droves. They scattered, screaming, into alleys and doorways, stumbling over the open gutters, crouching by walls. Then, in a new wave of panic, they began running again."

The shooting lasted all night. The few reporters there said that more than three thousand demonstrators were killed, including children and monks. Others claimed that as many as ten thousand died. People were proud and horrified at the same time. Similar demonstrations went on in almost every major town in Burma. Arrests and killings continued here and there until August 13, when finally Sein Lwin resigned. The government thought it could appease the people by changing leaders again. This time Dr. Maung Maung—reported to take a soft approach—was appointed. This tactic didn't work. People marched in protest day after day, growing bolder with each demonstration. "We actually thought we were winning against the government," said Khin Ohmar.

During these weeks of demonstrations, people discussed new forms of government. Some of the old politicians who had been in office at the time of independence got together to plan political strategies. Two former generals under Ne Win—Aung Gyi and Tin Oo—approached Aung San Suu Kyi and U Nu, the former prime minister. They discussed forming a democratic party. Although Suu Kyi had never held a

> I OBVIOUSLY HAD TO THINK ABOUT IT. BUT MY INSTINCT WAS 'THIS IS NOT A TIME WHEN ANYONE WHO CARES CAN STAY OUT.' AS MY FATHER'S DAUGHTER, I FELT I HAD A DUTY TO GET INVOLVED.

political office, many people believed she could inspire followers because she was Aung San's daughter. She knew critics would call her naïve and inexperienced. Still, she believed she could promote democracy and help create a unity of purpose in the people of Burma. The group asked Suu Kyi to give a speech, and she accepted. "I obviously had to think about it. But my instinct was 'this is not a time when anyone who cares can stay out.' As my father's daughter, I felt I had a duty to get involved."

Tin Oo (left) *and Kyi Maung meet with Suu Kyi at her house to discuss forming a democratic party.*

On August 25, people started to gather at the base of
the Shwedagon Pagoda in northern Rangoon for a huge
democratic rally the next day. At the Shwedagon, a place

The Shwedagon Pagoda, seen from the Royal Lakes

One of Suu Kyi's supporters wears thanaka, *a traditional Burmese face powder.*

of worship, the people of Burma have also met to express their political beliefs. On August 26, hundreds of thousands of people from all over Burma arrived. Word had spread that Aung San's daughter would address the crowds.

On August 26, 1988, Aung San Suu Kyi formally announced her support for the democracy movement. People listened carefully, wondering what the daughter of their national hero would say.

Aung San Suu Kyi speaks about democracy to the crowds at the Shwedagon Pagoda.

To the crowd at Shwedagon Pagoda, she spoke in Burmese. She opened her speech by asking people to be disciplined and united. She said her purpose was to show the people's wish for a multiparty democratic government. She then asked everyone to observe a moment of silence for the students who had lost their lives while trying to stand up for justice. She wanted listeners to share the good merit of the students' actions and sacrifice.

As she went on, she explained why she stood there before them and why she wanted to help her country: "It is true that I have lived abroad. It is also true that I am married to a foreigner. These facts have never interfered and will never interfere with or lessen my love and devotion for my country by any measure or degree."

She said that the present national crisis could not be ignored. She explained that she agreed with her father's opinion that democracy is the only political system that promotes and strengthens peace—the only political system that the people should aim for. "This national crisis could in fact be called the second struggle for national independence," she said.

> IT IS TRUE THAT I HAVE LIVED ABROAD. IT IS ALSO TRUE THAT I AM MARRIED TO A FOREIGNER. THESE FACTS HAVE NEVER INTERFERED AND WILL NEVER INTERFERE WITH OR LESSEN MY LOVE AND DEVOTION FOR MY COUNTRY.

The rest of her talk focused on peace and unity. She described how her father had built up the army to protect the Burmese people—now citizens and the army should unite to make the country strong. She also talked about the split between the young and the old, the students and the politicians. She asked her audience to forgive past mistakes and to open a dialogue, to bring about political freedom in a multiparty system. She asked that the country hold free elections so the people could quickly regain confidence in their government.

Before the speech, many people had not understood their rights. In her clear words, Suu Kyi taught listeners the concept of democracy. Some listeners did not like her idea of uniting with the murderous army, but they respected her nonetheless. Older people sat amazed at how much Suu Kyi resembled her father. She impressed them with her vigor and her clarity and with her call for peace, her call against violence. Suu Kyi gave new energy to the movement for democracy. Through early September, many people felt a sense of purpose.

On September 18, 1988, the army rolled back into Rangoon. They had had enough of the demonstrations and open criticism of the government. Over the radio, the army announced a curfew from six o'clock in the evening until six in the morning. They forbade protest and threatened to deal harshly with all demonstrators. For two days, the army attacked public gatherings.

General Saw Maung took over the government. He called the new government the State Law and Order Restoration Council (SLORC). General Saw Maung pronounced himself prime minister, foreign minister, and defense minister all at the same time. He promised that Burma's one-party rule would end, and that the country would hold national elections. In a September 23 radio broadcast to the nation, he told listeners that SLORC did not plan to hold state power for long. He explained that the army meant only "to maintain law and order, provide secure and smooth transportation, improve conditions of food, clothing, and shelter to the people, and hold multiparty elections." Within the next months, more than two hundred parties registered.

Even so, most people believed that Ne Win was still acting head of the government. The tactics were familiar. Although SLORC officially allowed parties to form, it did plenty to wipe out grassroot activities. It forbade unauthorized publications and declared its *Working People's Daily* the only legal newspaper. This was SLORC's way to keep parties from spreading information and political ideas. And the army mowed down the citizens it was meant to protect.

The military threats felt extremely menacing. Many citizens were again afraid to discuss politics. Students fled to the country's borders with India, Bangladesh, Thailand, Tibet and China; some joined armed resistance fighters defending the ethnic groups. And the government started its cleanup act. It hunted down freedom fighters and arrested them, keeping dissension off the streets.

On September 24, the pro-democracy movement created the National League for Democracy (NLD). It named Aung Gyi as chairman, Tin Oo as vice chairman, and Aung San Suu Kyi as general secretary. She quickly became the favorite party representative. Soon, NLD leaders began to travel and campaign for national elections.

To tell the people in rural Burma about the democracy movement, Suu Kyi went to towns and villages throughout the country by boat, train, car, and bicycle. She often wore ethnic clothing as a way of showing solidarity with non-Burman groups. Her many speeches were translated into ethnic languages, and she demonstrated to the people that she was working for complete national unity, just as her father had done. People loved her. Crowds of smiling people often surrounded her—all handing her garlands of flowers or trying to talk to her.

The government also arrested many NLD organizers along with leaders of a student-led party. The head of this party fled the country before he could be arrested. He joined another student party at the Thai border, which linked itself with ethnic rebels. The students and ethnic freedom fighters armed themselves against SLORC. They no longer believed that peaceful negotiations could work.

The NLD did not support armed resistance. Suu Kyi and her colleagues continued their campaign—promoting peace, discipline, and responsibility. Although SLORC

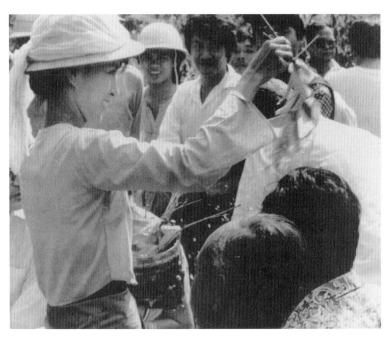

In a traditional new year's ceremony, Suu Kyi sprinkles water over the heads of her followers.

made great efforts to obstruct the NLD and told locals not to go out and greet Suu Kyi during campaigns, support for the democratic party grew stronger. Some SLORC soldiers even climbed down from their military trucks to listen to Suu Kyi's speeches.

"Among all the politicians who had emerged or re-emerged on the Burmese scene since August 1988, Aung San Suu Kyi stood out as the only one who could unify all segments of Burmese society: the urban as well as the rural population, the young student radicals and the older, much more moderate pro-democracy advocates."

Although Suu Kyi was now thoroughly involved in the democracy movement, she still cared for her mother, who was failing quickly. On December 27, 1988, Daw Khin Kyi died at the age of seventy-five. On January 2, 1989, more than one hundred thousand people came out to watch her funeral procession and show respect to Daw Khin Kyi and Aung San Suu Kyi. Suu Kyi had made a public plea for calm and discipline, and there were no disturbances that day.

On June 18, 1989, SLORC decided that the name Burma should no longer be used. In the Burmese language, the country is called *Myanmar Naing-ngan.* According to SLORC, the name *Myanmar* should be used in English instead of *Burma.* The Burmese people had no control over the name change and are offended when the country is not called Burma in English.

By July 1989, the tension between SLORC and its opponents was even stronger. The government announced

that national elections would be held in the spring of
1990, and the Burmese set their goal for a new government. Suu Kyi openly criticized Ne Win for mastermind-
ing the economic demise of the country. Rumors spread
that SLORC would gun her down.

Suu Kyi continued to campaign, and SLORC stepped
up its interference of her public talks. Once, SLORC ordered a group of NLD supporters to disband and refrain
from blocking the road. Suu Kyi claimed that it was
SLORC who was blocking the road, and she would not
back down. Suu Kyi then asked her supporters to stay behind, and she walked alone through the crowds toward
the guns that were aimed at her. Before the captain, Myint
Oo, could give an order to fire at Suu Kyi, a major inter-
vened and ordered the men to lower their guns. Myint Oo
was promoted for his planned attack of Suu Kyi.

For July 19, 1989, the anniversary of her father's assassination, Suu Kyi had planned a march to Aung San's
tomb near the Shwedagon Pagoda. Before the march took
place, however, SLORC threatened to imprison or execute
anyone who opposed the government. It set up road-
blocks, cut telephone lines to foreign countries, and sta-
tioned thousands of soldiers along Rangoon's roads. Suu
Kyi had to cancel her march to avoid another massacre.

On July 20, SLORC finally took action to cripple the
NLD. Soldiers surrounded Suu Kyi's home, put her under
house arrest, arrested the students in her compound, and
took Tin Oo, who had become the NLD chairman, to In-
sein prison. The voices of the NLD were muffled.

Khin Nyunt, SLORC's chief of secret police, defended the government's action against the NLD by saying that the democratic party was being manipulated by communist rebels. Although he gave little evidence for his accusations, Khin Nyunt later claimed that the NLD had plotted with foreign powers to uproot SLORC.

Many foreign democratic governments, including the United States, immediately condemned SLORC's human rights violations. They also stopped all assistance to Burma's military government as long as it continued to violate human rights. The end of funding became a big problem for SLORC. The country depended on foreign aid and investment, but SLORC did not want foreigners to interfere in its internal politics. So SLORC did what it could to disguise human rights violations and declare most political groups as threats to national security. In addition, SLORC distributed literature accusing Aung San Suu Kyi of corruption and moral weakness. One pamphlet even made the fabricated claim that she had multiple husbands.

At the same time that SLORC was fighting democratic groups in Burma's cities, it was also waging war against ethnic freedom fighters in many of Burma's border areas. Many of the ethnic groups did not follow the fledgling political parties in Rangoon. Instead they armed themselves and stood against SLORC's troops. The ethnic groups fought for their own rights and liberty in their territories.

Suu Kyi was confined to her childhood home by the military government in the summer of 1989.

LIVING BEHIND BARBED WIRE

IN THE SUMMER OF 1989, AUNG SAN SUU KYI began her life under house arrest. Guards surrounded her compound, and only her maid, Maria, went in and out. After Michael, Alexander, and Kim returned to England in September, Suu Kyi was truly cut off from the world.

At first, she was not allowed to see her family, but she dreamed about them. She struggled with this separation, but she reminded herself that her sons were well loved and cared for by their father. She also had confidence that her marriage would survive. From the beginning, she disciplined herself so she would not feel depressed.

Michael understood his wife's determination. "She is prepared to remain in detention until there is reform in her country," he said.

By denying Suu Kyi access to her family, SLORC had hoped to force her to leave the country. Although she was dedicated to Michael, Alexander, and Kim, and she was

During house arrest, Suu Kyi meditated, read, and listened to the news.

free to rejoin them in Oxford, Suu Kyi would not turn away from Burma. She believed that nobody should relax in happiness when so many people were suffering. "Here is a woman who easily could have left the country, gone back and lived an idyllic life at Oxford University, and watched the maturing of her young sons into manhood, and had a wonderfully beautiful life with a man who loves her deeply. Yet, she has given that all up," said an expert on Burma. "She is one with the people in suffering. I don't think there is a Burman or minority who does

The presence of SLORC soldiers is noticeable in Rangoon.

not share with her and believe she is sharing with them. That's a tremendous strength that no soldier can match."

Alone in her Rangoon home, Suu Kyi set up a daily routine for herself to keep her mind and body strong. She only varied that routine on Saturday and Sunday, when she let herself enjoy leisurely activity. At four-thirty each morning, she rose and tidied herself up. Then she sat in a half-lotus position—legs crossed with one foot up on the opposite thigh—at the foot of her bed. There she meditated by concentrating on her breathing and being aware of everything around her.

This practice, called insight meditation, helped her to become focused and calm and to understand her mental habits. As a Buddhist, Suu Kyi had learned to observe herself "from outside" and to recognize her own imperfections of character. Daily meditation during house arrest helped her understand herself even better. "Perhaps my great aunt helped me to cultivate self-awareness," she said. "I have always been aware of my faults, so nothing has come as a shock to me. But, house arrest has given me the opportunity to try to overcome my own weaknesses and faults, especially through meditation. . . . I am very short-tempered, but I think I am far less short-tempered now than I used to be."

At five-thirty, Suu Kyi turned on her shortwave radio and listened to the British Broadcast Corporation (BBC) World Service news. At six o'clock, she heard the *Voice of America* Burmese-language broadcast, followed by the

. . . there was no . . . real rule of law when laws in shape of ordinances and the appeared suddenly, like rabbit a conjurer's hat, at the will o dividual or a dictating grou

JAWAHARLAL NEHRU.

Suu Kyi posted sayings of her father and Nehru where the SLORC guards had to see them as they came and went.

BBC Burmese-language program. Finally at seven o'clock, she listened to the *Democratic Voice of Burma,* broadcast from Norway. "So by the time I had breakfast quite late at nine, I was almost fully aware of what was going on in the outside world," she said.

After listening to news, Suu Kyi exercised. She did aerobics or spent twenty minutes on her NordicTrack. Before eating breakfast of fruit, occasionally an egg, and tea or milk, Suu Kyi bathed and sometimes read Buddhist writings. The rest of the day she spent reading, studying, eating simple meals of fish and rice, and listening to evening radio news. She often took another bath before bed.

Although she enjoyed writing, she wrote little because she did not want SLORC to raid her premises again and take her writings. People sent her many books, so she did not run out of reading material. Her husband gave her a set of the Encyclopedia Britannica. "I read a lot of biographies. They taught me how other people faced problems in life. Mandela. Sakharov. Mother Teresa. People felt they had to send me books about people who were in prison."

There were times in her detention when Suu Kyi had no money for food. Her usual weight of 106 pounds dropped below 100, and her hair fell out. With the help of her one government liaison officer—a lieutenant colonel in Burma's military intelligence—and her maid, Maria, she made arrangements with SLORC to sell her furniture for money to cover her living expenses. Suu Kyi received money for the furniture, but SLORC did not tell her that they had only stored her belongings. Later SLORC offered to give the items back, but Suu Kyi said she would not take them as a gift. She would buy them back.

While Suu Kyi remained under house arrest, SLORC agreed to go ahead with the national election in 1990. Before the vote, SLORC formally disqualified Aung San Suu Kyi's candidacy because, SLORC claimed, she committed a crime against national security. Its claim was that Aung San Suu Kyi "had been influenced by anti-government, opportunistic politicians and insurgent groups in their attempt to seize political power for their own end. . . . For her own good and for the good of the country she had to be restrained in order to prevent her from promoting the cause of these unsavory political elements who found their way and got themselves into positions of influence around her to create disunity among the only unified establishment left in the country, the [military], which was endeavouring to stabilize the situation created by the political vacuum."

In the 1990 election, more than 2,300 candidates, representing ninety-three political parties, ran for 485 assembly seats. Some independent reports said that the election was fair. However, many people disputed this assessment by pointing out that the favorite candidate, Aung San Suu Kyi, was under house arrest, and that the military had often tried to hamper campaigning.

In a letter, Suu Kyi described her campaign to Michael: "All the way, people had been told not to go out of their houses, not to wave, etc., and gunshots had been fired to frighten them."

Some Westerners in Burma during the election reported that many Burmese citizens did not know how or where to vote. The military government did little to help the public, and they patrolled cities in convoys to stop public gatherings in the street. Public gatherings of five or more people was still illegal.

One foreign diplomat in Rangoon at election time, made the following comment. "You wouldn't know a campaign is on if it weren't for the official newspapers. The town is dead. . . . There is a mixture of fear and defiance among the Burmese."

Fair or not, the elections took place on May 27, 1990.

Even though they are not allowed to vote, Buddhist monks wait for the early returns of the election in 1990.

To SLORC's great surprise, the National League for
Democracy won 392 out of the 485 seats contested,
eighty-one percent of the elected assembly. The National
Unity Party—SLORC's party—won only ten seats. The remaining eighty-three seats went to ethnic leaders, most of
whom were anti-SLORC. There was no question about
which party the people wanted running the government.

Despite the strong election results, SLORC refused to
hand over power to the NLD. They made plenty of ex-
cuses. They told the public that the election was meant
to provide the country with delegates who could write
a new constitution. And SLORC insisted that until the
constitution was written and adopted, no new government could take over. On June 19, 1990, SLORC's General Saw Maung announced that the transfer of power
would not be quick, and the drafting of the constitution
would be complicated. True to Saw Maung's promise,
SLORC moved slowly on the constitution. Although
Major General Myo Nyunt denied delaying the power
transfer, SLORC left the constitution unfinished for
many years.

In early August 1990, Burma was filled with more unrest. People were agitated by SLORC's power theft. On
the second anniversary of the 1988 uprising, monks and
students in Mandalay demonstrated. The government
put down this resistance and killed two monks and two
students. It blamed the NLD for the political disruption,
and it arrested pro-democracy demonstrators all over the
country. Among those arrested were six acting leaders of

the NLD. By now, SLORC had cut off both the first and the second levels of NLD leadership.

During this unrest, eight elected members of the NLD, including Aung San Suu Kyi's cousin, Dr. Sein Win—whose father was assassinated at the same time as General Aung San—fled to Burma's border, to an area under the control of the Karen Liberation Union. In their headquarters at Manerplaw, on December 18, 1990, these members established the National Coalition Government of the Union of Burma (NCGUB).

This coalition hoped to keep the democracy movement alive while the NLD was being toppled by SLORC. Sein Win was chosen to be prime minister. From Manerplaw, Sein Win and the NCGUB tried to contact foreign governments for support for Burma. Although foreigners were sympathetic, no great actions were taken against SLORC. Later, after a trip outside of Thailand, Sein Win was refused reentry into Thailand, and he was stranded in exile. In October 1993, he set up an NCGUB office in Washington, D.C. On January 26, 1995, Manerplaw fell to SLORC forces.

During the months that followed the national election, pro-democracy advocates formed several political coalitions and organizations. This created many splits in the anti-SLORC movement. Some democracy advocates joined forces with rebel armies who would continue to fight SLORC troops in the years to come. But SLORC countered these moves by arresting hundreds of citizens, including at least 64 of the leaders elected in 1990.

In another move to push back its opposition, SLORC returned to smearing Aung San Suu Kyi's reputation. It stated that because Suu Kyi was married to a foreigner, she, as leader, would be a national risk. The State Law and Order Restoration Council feared she could leak state secrets to foreigners. So it planned to write a constitutional regulation forbidding national leaders to be married to foreigners.

In 1991, Michael Aris edited a collection of Suu Kyi's writings and added those of Burmese scholars and family friends. These essays became a book entitled *Freedom from Fear and Other Writings,* which was printed in England. The royalties from this book were deposited into Suu Kyi's bank account in Rangoon, and her maid was able to withdraw from it when Suu Kyi needed something.

Suu Kyi was neither bored nor lonely under house arrest. She taught her guards to speak a little English and discussed her views on democracy with them. So SLORC rotated the guards often. From time to time, she had conversations with her military liaison. She treated him like a visitor, and they often discussed such topics as food and politics. She felt sure that he reported their conversations back to SLORC. Suu Kyi always hoped she would be able to talk directly to SLORC. She welcomed an honest invitation for negotiation.

Although Suu Kyi rarely discussed her moments of weakness, she openly admitted her anguish over the fate of her student supporters. Several times she cried for them. She knew, however, that it would not help to worry. She tried to remain positive, and she sent them blessings through her meditations.

Despite the barbed wire around her house and withering garden, Suu Kyi didn't feel imprisoned, at least not in her mind. She hardly noticed the soldiers outside. Because she was unafraid of what SLORC would do to her, she felt free.

Although Suu Kyi had only limited contact with people outside her gates, the rest of the world did not forget her.

Alexander (center) *and Kim accept the Nobel Peace Prize for their mother.*

She was honored with over twenty humanitarian awards, including the prestigious Sakharov Prize for Freedom of Thought and the Nobel Prize for peace, both in 1991. After the announcement of the Nobel, which had to be accepted by Suu Kyi's sons, newspapers, radio stations, and television networks all carried stories about the strong-minded Burmese leader who had been shut away in her crumbling colonial home in her little-known country.

Suu Kyi also earned money from several of these humanitarian awards, but she set aside that money for her people. She wanted it to be used to upgrade the health and education of Burmese people.

The Nobel Prize affected Suu Kyi's situation in both positive and negative ways. Because of the publicity, many people throughout the world began to rally for Suu Kyi's freedom. Student activists, some of whom had fled to Western countries, organized demonstrations. Burmese exiles, who mourned the state of their country, also joined forces and tried to bring media attention to Burma. A British film director, John Boorman, began making a film called *Beyond Rangoon,* which took place in Burma and focused on SLORC's cruel suppression of the democracy movement during the unrest of 1988.

At the same time, SLORC was angered by the honor of the Nobel Prize bestowed to its enemy. Although Suu Kyi might have had a chance to negotiate with SLORC before the Nobel announcement, after the news became public, SLORC did not want to appear weak to foreigners. They kept their hard line against Suu Kyi.

On December 28, 1991, Khin Nyunt announced that SLORC would never allow Aung San Suu Kyi to become a national leader. In the same month, SLORC put pressure on the remaining members of the NLD. They were forced to expel Aung San Suu Kyi from the party. By the end of the next month, the NLD also had to expel Tin Oo, who was still in prison. Many NLD members were furious over these moves and called the actions illegal.

After 1991, SLORC accelerated its destruction of political opposition, and increased commercial production without paying Burmese workers. The government relied on an unpaid work force as a means of amassing more profits, but it claimed that Burmese people volunteered their labor as a noble act of charity. So SLORC made the following statement about volunteer community work: "It has always been a tradition in Myanmar culture to donate labour in the building of pagodas, monasteries, roads and bridges and in the digging and clearing of wells, ponds, dams, and canals. A belief exists that doing so leads to mental and physical well-being....This is all part of community work that raises the standard of living, both materially and spiritually....The local populace is already enjoying the benefits of their own endeavours."

Citizens who have worked for SLORC have secretly told their own story. Rural laborers have told Amnesty International, Human Rights Watch/Asia, Western journalists, and the Special Rapporteur of the United Nations that they were forced to work for SLORC or pay a large penalty. People denied that they volunteered to

Burmese workers build a road.

work and to provide the government with such items as pickaxes, mattocks, hoes, and tins of rice. In some districts of Burma, as much as eighty percent of the population was working without pay, and pregnant women and young children were part of the work force. Families were fined, imprisoned, or killed for not complying with the government's demands.

When SLORC wanted to relocate a village and use occupied land for a road, hotel, airport, or gas pipeline, government officers simply arrived in the village and

The government moved the entire population of Pagan, Burma, to make the ancient city more appealing to tourists.

announced their plans. The villagers had to move where SLORC demanded and work however SLORC wanted. Those who hid from SLORC could be shot or used as minesweepers to walk through fields checking for mines planted by opposition armies. Many men, women, and children lost limbs in the process. The people say they have no freedom.

In the 1990s, sixty percent of SLORC's money was funneled into buying military equipment from countries in Europe, Asia, and the former USSR. It also raised money by selling off much of Burma's gems, offering Thailand logging rights to teak forests, and taking profits from the illegal opium traffic. It then imported foreign tanks, aircraft, and guns, which it used against the Burmese people.

After SLORC quelled the pro-democracy movement, it increased its attack on Burma's ethnic groups and minorities, and used chemical weapons against the Kachin, Karen, and Mon groups. It developed a systematic ethnic cleansing by denying full citizenship to ethnic minority groups and forcing them to flee Burma. Since SLORC's rise to power in 1988, an estimated 500,000 people have fled across Burma's borders to live as refugees in exile.

In 1992, after Suu Kyi had been under house arrest for two and a half years, SLORC finally allowed Michael, Kim, and Alexander to visit. Suu Kyi was startled to see how much her sons had grown and changed during the separation. Of Kim, she was most surprised: "When I saw my younger son again for the first time after a separation of two years and seven months he had changed from a round faced not-quite-twelve-year-old into a rather stylish 'cool' teen-ager. If I had met him in the street I would not have known him for my little son."

In December 1992, a group of Nobel Peace Prize winners, including the Dalai Lama, Oscar Arias, Bishop Desmond Tutu, and Betty Williams tried to enter Burma to see Suu Kyi. Their visa applications were rejected. So they flew into Thailand instead and made a public plea for her release.

During her detention, Suu Kyi developed into the political prisoner often described in newspaper articles that she never read. "I was under house arrest because of my politics," she said, "so politics became my whole life. Most of the time, I spent thinking about politics.... Once you're alone as a political prisoner, then politics is your whole existence." She tried not to wonder at length about the welfare of her family, so she turned her mind to the welfare of young political prisoners who needed a protector. She also developed ideas for a future, compassionate government of Burma.

By 1994, SLORC was looking hard for international funds to upgrade its military arsenal. It also wanted to modernize the country and open it to foreign tourists. In order to interest private investors and obtain loans from foreign governments, SLORC had to show its tolerance of political controversy and publicly change its treatment of its famous prisoner, Suu Kyi. The government finally allowed Suu Kyi a visitor who hoped to negotiate her release.

*Seen through the barbed wire surrounding Suu Kyi's home, a huge
new hotel encourages tourism.*

United States Congressman Bill Richardson from New
Mexico was Suu Kyi's first nonfamily visitor. He felt priv-
ileged to meet such "a woman of great stature—a Nobel
Prize winner—enormously bright, engaging." Richardson
believed that by allowing him to talk to Suu Kyi, SLORC
was trying to "send a positive humanitarian gesture to the
[U.S.] president." According to Richardson, SLORC also
wanted unofficial access to President Bill Clinton.

Richardson reported that Suu Kyi appeared thin and tense, and that she mentioned having a back problem because of nutritional deficiencies. "She seemed to be under a lot of pressure because she was having difficulty getting access to her children and her husband. She said she particularly missed her children," he said.

Despite her sparse household, Suu Kyi refused any of the conveniences that Richardson offered to arrange for her. Suu Kyi told Richardson that she wanted only an open, honest dialogue with SLORC, nothing else. "The main thrust of her message to the world, and to me," he said, "was despite the physical and mental discomforts to her, and the loss of seeing her children grow up, the most important facet of her life was standing up for democracy for the people of Burma, and not surrendering her principles by agreeing to have luxuries and other advantages that the SLORC had offered her."

Suu Kyi's family and supporters had little hope that their hero would be released upon the end of her six-year sentence. They believed that SLORC would come up with another reason for detaining her, as they had done in the past. Human rights activists around the world organized media campaigns and demonstrations to observe Suu Kyi's fiftieth birthday on June 19, 1995, and to call for her release. The world watched.

Released from house arrest on July 10, 1995, Aung San Suu Kyi is elated.

∎

UNENDING COMPASSION

IN 1995, INTERNATIONAL VOICES FOR FREEDOM cried out about the abuses in Burma. Nobel Prize laureates, Amnesty International, the International Committee of the Red Cross, foreign politicians, student activists, and non-governmental agencies all voiced frustration with SLORC's policies, and with Suu Kyi's continued detention.

Finally, SLORC was forced to take a step to quell the criticism. In an unannounced move on July 10, 1995, SLORC released Aung San Suu Kyi. It said that the release was "unconditional"—a term that led people to believe that Suu Kyi could do whatever she wanted, whenever she wanted, and that she made no deals to gain her freedom. Although SLORC reported nothing about Suu Kyi's freedom in Burma's news, the international media was immediately flooded. Suu Kyi's family, friends, and followers all over the world were stunned and overjoyed.

The next day hundreds of jubilant supporters crowded

the sidewalk outside Suu Kyi's compound gate. People cheered and cried at the same time. Traffic along University Avenue moved slowly past her house. Despite SLORC's continued ban on public gathering, people waited to hear the first public words of their beloved leader. They even brought small children to witness this important moment in Burma's history.

Burmese people crowd the street outside of Suu Kyi's compound to hear her speak.

Suu Kyi speaks to the waiting crowd.

Standing on a table steadied on top of a desk, Suu Kyi positioned herself where all could see her, and addressed the crowd. "We will produce the form of government that the people want. . . . But at the same time, we must not be reckless. We will surely get to our destination if we join hands. We will not bear grudges against anybody else. We have to try to understand each other."

As soon as Suu Kyi was released, she began meeting with her former colleagues. People came and went from her compound all day long and into the night. Suu Kyi expressed her thanks to SLORC for releasing her, but she warned her supporters and foreign governments that her release was not a guarantee that SLORC would change its policies. She advised investors and politicians to wait and watch the political climate in her country before planning reconciliation or investment in Burma. "I would like them [foreign governments] to see it [my release] as a good sign, as a hopeful sign, but I would like them to regard this with caution. Cautious optimism is what is called for."

Another Nobel Peace Prize winner, the Dalai Lama of Tibet, commented on Suu Kyi's release: "Of course the release is a good thing, but the question is about *real* change. I don't think any real change has happened yet. Now with her release, outside voices can be more effective. Aung San Suu Kyi will make a contribution not only for Burma—for her own people—but internationally as well."

When President Clinton of the United States heard the good news, he made a strong statement about future stability in Burma: Suu Kyi's release could be "a major milestone towards the restoration of peace and stability in Burma [if it] enables her to participate freely in a genuine process of political reconciliation."

Politicians and friends around the world speculated about Suu Kyi's release. They were taken off guard, and they wondered what had triggered SLORC to let her free. Some believed SLORC felt so powerful that Suu Kyi's freedom was no longer a threat. Others believed SLORC was trying to escape more shame.

One Burmese man living in exile in the United States wrote about Suu Kyi's release: "In releasing Aung San Suu Kyi from six years of house arrest, Burma's ruling junta could no longer withstand the shame, or as we say in Burmese, 'the face got hot' from international outcry against its human rights record."

In the first seven months after her release, Suu Kyi left Rangoon only once. She went to see a well-respected Buddhist monk. Although she has been invited to give public talks and to receive awards in many foreign countries, Suu Kyi has decided not to leave Burma. She and her colleagues believe that SLORC would deny her reentry into her country. Although SLORC called Suu Kyi's release unconditional, SLORC still denies her full liberty in her political work and in her private affairs. In February and March of 1996, SLORC twice prevented Suu Kyi from traveling within Burma. The government also arrested actors who performed a political parody at Suu Kyi's home. During the Burmese New Year's festival, the military blocked off University Avenue in front of Suu Kyi's compound and kept people from attending Suu Kyi's celebration. In May 1996, SLORC denied Michael, Alexander, and Kim entrance visas to Burma.

Suu Kyi spends most of her time in her compound. Her daily routine has changed drastically since her release. Instead of studying constantly and listening to news, she receives visitors regularly, gives weekly public talks to supporters outside her gate, holds press conferences and private interviews, writes speeches, and makes plans

Suu Kyi talks with an NLD supporter who was crippled in prison.

with her NLD colleagues. Suu Kyi's Saturdays are no longer ones of leisure, but Sundays are usually, not always, days of calm. "I can linger over my breakfast cup of tea. I can even read while sipping my tea. I can bathe and wash my hair without haste and I can tidy up the mess that has accumulated over the week."

Suu Kyi may take her time on Sunday mornings, but by the afternoon she must prepare and then deliver her four o'clock public address. After the public meeting, she sits with friends and colleagues, who bring snacks of glutinous rice and fried fish, and they exchange news. She has a chance to be relaxed and laugh with her beloved friends. Nightfall comes quickly, and Suu Kyi has but a short sleep before her work starts again. Hers is

Tin Oo and Kyi Maung join Suu Kyi as she walks to her gate to give her weekly speech.

a loaded schedule, but she does not feel burdened for two reasons: "First, I have dedicated and honorable (and good humored) colleagues whom I can trust and respect, and second, I gather strength from each day satisfactorily accounted for, including the brief days of rest, which I would like to think well-earned."

On October 9, 1995, the NLD convened and voted to reinstate Suu Kyi as the party's general secretary. The party has quietly organized a strong political network that acts by democratic process.

Because SLORC is losing ground with its failing economic policies, Suu Kyi and many others believe that it will crumble some day. Suu Kyi is confident that the NLD's cause will prevail because a great majority of people in Burma want democracy. The NLD wants to be ready and organized to provide Burma with a governmental system that includes political, administrative, and social branches, and that has legal, health, and educational committees. The NLD also wants to establish a sound legal system based on firm principles of justice. Suu Kyi talks openly about her vision of democracy: "We want a better democracy, a fuller democracy with compassion and loving kindness. . . . We should not be ashamed about talking about loving kindness and compassion in political terms. Values like love and compassion should be part of politics because justice must always be tempered by mercy. We prefer the word 'compassion.' That is warmer and more tender than 'mercy.'"

> VALUES LIKE LOVE AND COMPASSION SHOULD BE PART OF POLITICS BECAUSE JUSTICE MUST ALWAYS BE TEMPERED BY . . . COMPASSION.

Immediately after her release, Suu Kyi and the NLD advocated waiting and planning instead of striking out quickly against SLORC. They hoped for calm discussions with SLORC and the ethnic leaders. On February

25, 1996, Suu Kyi told reporters that the Burmese people could stay calm and not act hastily. "The Burmese people know how to bide their time. They know when they have to wait. They know when they have to act."

Although Burmese citizens are accustomed to restraint, stress, oppression, and self-denial, they still hold on to some hope of change. In clandestine ways, people express their disgust with the present regime and their wish for democracy. Although not everyone believes Aung San Suu Kyi can defeat SLORC, many people risk their freedom to tell foreigners about their support for her. "Everyone loves her except the government," said one young woman in Rangoon.

An elderly, educated Rangoon merchant, sighing heavily and spying at the corners outside his shop, confirmed reports of frustration and despair. "We have lived under so much stress. We don't know peace. We know how to behave. We have to see the good as fate and the bad as fate. Since the Japanese occupation, we have had nothing—a half century wasted. Aung San Suu Kyi and the government are banging heads. We need peace."

Aung San Suu Kyi and the NLD repeatedly called for a dialogue with SLORC. Suu Kyi said that national reconciliation could be achieved if a meeting were held with SLORC, the NLD, and the ethnic minority leaders. Suu Kyi believes that sooner or later all broken governments must settle their problems at the negotiating table instead of on the battlefield. Suu Kyi still questions how long SLORC will hold out before negotiating peacefully.

In the meantime, Suu Kyi publicizes the problems in her country and looks for assistance from international allies. She asks foreigners to put themselves in the shoes of the Burmese and to ask themselves how they would feel if they were deprived of all rights. She asks foreign governments not to invest in Burma until the aid can be used to benefit citizens and not the SLORC generals.

Suu Kyi says she is not angry at SLORC, but that she wishes they would "hurry up and do something for the Burmese people." As far as she can see, the rising inflation, the declining standards of education, and the dismal state of Burma's health care all indicate a failing economy and a misuse of power. Although SLORC has built dozens of modern, deluxe hotels to house tourists and investors, Suu Kyi does not see this construction as a mark of a booming country, but of a greedy, narrow-minded government.

In May 1996, the NLD called together a conference of democracy party members, many of whom were elected in the 1990 elections. Seven days before the beginning of the meeting, to be held at Suu Kyi's compound, SLORC arrested 238 conference delegates and unknown numbers of other party members. Despite the arrests, Aung San Suu Kyi held the meeting to step up party action toward democracy. Only eighteen delegates escaped arrest and attended the conference.

Suu Kyi boldly announced the NLD's plans to draft a constitution separate from the one debated in the SLORC-controlled congress. By writing a constitution, the elected representatives could offer citizens a system organized around human rights and justice. This step was the NLD's strongest yet against the oppressive military force. In response, SLORC staged mass rallies of government employees to denounce Suu Kyi and cheer for the military government. Most people believe the employees were forced to rally against Suu Kyi.

Aung San Suu Kyi has unending compassion for her nation. She worries a great deal about the hearts and minds of the people in Burma. "I would like a bit more

Burmese people celebrate the new year's water festival.

security for the people. I don't want the people to worry about where their next meal is coming from. I want them to have, at least, a basic sense of security—that they have enough to eat, a roof to live under, and that they're not going to be pulled away and put in jail just because the authorities are angry with them."

THE FUTURE OF COURSE IS DEMOCRACY FOR BURMA. IT IS GOING TO HAPPEN, AND I'M GOING TO BE HERE WHEN IT HAPPENS.

Suu Kyi's immediate goals are to empower her countrymen and women, and to bring modernization to all levels of society in Burma. Toward that goal, she reflects on the power of democracy, and she brings her ideas to an open table of leaders and citizens who want to unite to free Burma. "The future of course is democracy for Burma," Suu Kyi says. "It is going to happen, and I'm going to be here when it happens."

S O U R C E S

p.9 Interview with author, Rangoon, 30 Nov. 1995.

p.10 Ibid.

p.10 Ibid.

p.10 Ibid.

p.11 Ibid.

p.12 Aung San Suu Kyi, *Freedom from Fear* (London: Penguin, 1991), xxi.

p.15 Aung San, *Burma's Challenge, 1946* (Rangoon: New Light of Burma, 1946), 109.

pp.19–20 Hugh Tinker, Andrew Griffin, and S. Ashton, *Burma: The Struggle for Independence, 1944–1948* (London: H.M.S.O., 1983–1984), 228.

p.23 Bertil Lintner, *Burma in Revolt* (Boulder, Colorado: Westview Press, 1994), xiii.

p.25 Barbara Bradley, "Dark Victory," *Vogue,* Oct. 1995, 377.

p.26 Interview with author, Rangoon, 30 Nov. 1995.

p.27 Aung San Suu Kyi, *Freedom,* 246.

p.28 Ibid.

p.29 Interview with author, Rangoon, 30 Nov. 1995.

pp.29–30 Edward Klein, "The Lady Triumphs," *Vanity Fair,* Oct. 1995, 131.

p.30 Ibid.

p.31 Ivan Suvanjieff, "You Could Start by Convincing a Friend," *Shambala Sun,* Jan. 1996, 33.

p.31 Interview with author, Rangoon, 30 Nov. 1995.

p.32 Ibid.

p.33 Suvanjieff, "You Could Start by Convincing a Friend," 33.

p.40 Klein, "The Lady Triumphs," 134.

p.43 Aung San Suu Kyi, *Freedom,* 212.

p.48 Ibid., 250.

p.53 Bradley, "Dark Victory," 320.

p.54 Aung San Suu Kyi, *Freedom,* xvii.

p.55 Anonymous letter to author, 10 Jan. 1996.

p.57 Aung San Suu Kyi, *Freedom,* 262.

p.57 Ibid., 264.

p.57 Marlee Clymer, "Shining Hope of Burma is Leader's Daughter," *El Paso Times,* 9 April 1989, 4F.

p.58 Interview with author, Rangoon, 30 Nov. 1995.

p.59 Anonymous letter to author, 29 Jan. 1996.

p.62 Anonymous interview with author, 29 Sept. 1995.

p.65 Interview with author, 8 Oct. 1995.

p.65 Ibid.

p.65 Interview with author, 29 Sept. 1995.

p.68 Kin Oung, *Who Killed Aung San* (Bangkok: White Lotus, 1993), 73.

p.68 Aung San Suu Kyi, *Freedom,* xv.

p.72 Interview with author, Washington, DC, 14 Sept. 1995.

p.72 Telephone interview with author, 2 April 1996.

p.74 Telephone interview with author, 1 April 1996.

p.75 Lintner, *Burma in Revolt,* 277.

pp.77–78 Ibid., 278.

p.78 Telephone conversation with author, 24 Jan. 1996.

p.79 Steven Erlanger, *New York Times,* 11 Jan. 1989.

pp.82–83 Aung San Suu Kyi, *Freedom,* 199.

p.83 Ibid.

p.84 Marc Weller, ed., *Democracy and Politics in Burma: A Collection of Documents* (Thailand: National Coalition Government of the Union of Burma, 1993).

p.87 Lintner, *Burma in Revolt,* 302-303.

p.91 Philip Shenon, *New York Times,* 18 May 1992, A3.

pp.92–93 Josef Silverstein in the video, "The Prisoner," 1995.

p.94 Interview with author, Rangoon, 30 Nov. 1995.

p.95 Steve Weinman, "Beyond the Order of Detention," (BBC, Nov. 1995), 12–13.

p.95 Klein, "The Lady Triumphs," 143.

p.96 1995 Report of the Special Rapporteur on Myanmar to the UN Commission on Human Rights.

p.96 Aung San Suu Kyi, *Freedom,* 220.

p.97 Steve Erlanger, *New York Times,* 27 May 1990, 3.

p.103 Response of the Government of Myanmar to the Memo of the Special Rapporteur, Nov./Dec. 1995, 28.

pp.106–107 Aung San Suu Kyi, "Prison Walls Affect Those on the Outside, Too," *Mainichi Daily News,* 31 Dec. 1995.

p.107 ABC News, interview with Aung San Suu Kyi, July 1995.

p.108 Interview with author, 18 July 1995.

p.109 Ibid.

p.113 Philip Shenon, *New York Times,* 12 July 1995, A3.

p.114 Ibid.

p.114 Interview with author, Houston, 8 Aug. 1995.

p.114 Philip Shenon, *New York Times,* 12 July 1995, A3.

p.115 U Kyaw Win, letter to *Time Magazine,* 24 July 1995.

p.116 Aung San Suu Kyi, "Savoring the Peace of a Well-Earned Weekend," *Mainichi Daily News,* 4 March 1996.

p.117 Ibid.

p.118 Interview with author, Rangoon, 30 Nov. 1995.

p.119 Robert Horn, *Associated Press,* 25 Feb. 1996.

p.119 Conversation with author, 25 Nov. 1995.

p.119 Conversation with author, Rangoon, 28 Nov. 1995.

p.120 Interview with author, Rangoon, 30 Nov. 1995.

pp.121–122 Ibid.

p.122 Aung San Suu Kyi, interview by Reuters, 30 May 1996.

BIBLIOGRAPHY

Aung San. *Burma's Challenge, 1946.* Rangoon: New Light of Burma, 1946.

Aung San Suu Kyi. *Freedom from Fear.* London: Penguin, 1991.

Bradley, Barbara. "Dark Victory," *Vogue,* October 1995.

Kin Oung. *Who Killed Aung San.* Bangkok: White Lotus, 1993.

Klein, Edward. "The Lady Triumphs," *Vanity Fair,* October 1995.

Lintner, Bertil. *Burma in Revolt.* Boulder, CO: Westview Press, 1994.

Silverstein, Josef. *Burmese Politics: The Dilemma of National Unity.* New Brunswick, New Jersey: Rutgers University Press, 1980.

Suvanjieff, Ivan. "You Could Start by Convincing a Friend," *Shambala Sun,* January 1996.

Tinker, Hugh, Andrew Griffin, and S. Ashton. *Burma: The Struggle for Independence, 1944–1948,* Vol. 1. London: H.M.S.O., 1983–1984.

Weller, Marc, ed., *Democracy and Politics in Burma: A Collection of Documents.* Thailand: Government Printing Office of the National Coalition Government of the Union of Burma, 1993.

Interviews with Aung San Suu Kyi, Jenny Tun Aung, Simon Billenness, Kenton Clymer, Marlee Clymer, Bob Fuller, Khin Omar, U Kyaw Win, Nyi Nyi Aung, Bill Richardson, Inge Sargent, Dr. Sein Win, Zarni, and Zaw Zaw.

A B O U T   T H E   A U T H O R

Whitney Stewart loves to travel to Asia and interview compassionate leaders. She always collects questions from U.S. children for her interviews. In 1995 she flew to Burma to visit the country and interview Aung San Suu Kyi. She has also interviewed the 14th Dalai Lama of Tibet and Sir Edmund Hillary and written biographies of them. She lives with her husband and son in New Orleans.

P H O T O   A C K N O W L E D G M E N T S

The photographs are copyrighted by and reproduced with the permission of: Reuters/Jonathon Karp/Archive Photos, pp. 1, 8; Wolfgang Kaehler, pp. 2–3; G. Fenmore, pp. 3, 113; Michelle Burgess, pp. 6–7, 80; AP/Wide World Photos, pp. 11, 34, 76, 77, 81, 97, 101; Reuters/Bettmann, p. 13; Burma Project USA, pp. 14, 17, 21, 30; Aung San Suu Kyi, pp. 18, 22, 28, 39, 46, 52, 56; Mr. Bilal Raschid, pp. 24, 63; Archive Photos, pp. 27, 41, 50; Bob Fuller, pp. 33, 42; UPI/Corbis-Bettmann, pp. 36, 66; Archive Photos/Camera Press, p. 37; The Bettmann Archive, p. 44; United Nations, p. 49; U Kyaw Win, pp. 58, 61, 62, 64; Reuters/Archive Photos, pp. 70, 82; Reuters/Richard Rothhass/Archive Photos, p. 73; Leslie Kean/Burma Project USA, pp. 79, 92, 93, 94, 108, 112, 116, 117; Reuters/David Brunnstrom/Archive Photos, p. 86; Whitney Stewart, pp. 90, 128; Luke Golobitsh, pp. 104, 121; Nevada Wier, p. 105; Corbis-Bettmann, p. 110.

Front cover photograph is by G. Fenmore.

DATE DUE			

**92
AUN**

**32751100308212
Stewart, Whitney.**

**Aung San Suu Kyi :
fearless voice of
Burma**

**BRUNSWICK GARDENS MDL SCHOOL
BOSTON PUBLIC SCHOOLS**